# LIVING WITH VOICES

An autobiography

## Arthur Oldham

Foreword by
Donald Mitchell

D1637813

## Thames Publishing

Distribution by William Elkin Music Services

Publisher and author acknowledge with grateful thanks the financial contribution made by the Britten Estate towards the publication of this book.

Printed and bound in Great Britain by
**Lonsdale Press**

# Contents

*Photographs between pages 32 and 33; 64 and 65*

# *Acknowledgements*

My thanks are due to:

- Claudine Duclos, my faithful assistant for more than 20 years, who first urged me to write this book;

- My wife, who sustained and encouraged me throughout;

- Raymond Vennier, for his beautiful photography;

- Donald Mitchell, for his gracious foreword and for his support generally; and

- John Bishop, my editor, whose wisdom and vast experience have been invaluable to me.

*    *    *

The quotations from the letters of Benjamin Britten, also the musical quotation from *This Way to the Tomb*, are © copyright the Trustees of the Britten-Pears Foundation and may not be further reproduced without the written permission of the Trustees.

# *Foreword*

Many readers of this remarkable autobiography will be thoroughly familiar with the name of Arthur Oldham, perhaps in particular as a most distinguished chorus master. The titles of the concluding chapters tell their own story: they include, most notably, the Edinburgh Festival Chorus, from 1965 to 1994, the choruses of the London Symphony Orchestra and the Concertgebouw Orchestra of Amsterdam, and, since its foundation by him in 1976, the chorus of the Orchestre de Paris; this last is a post he still holds. All else apart, it is a fascinating record of a musician who has made a distinctive contribution to the Europe that these days occupies more and more of our attention, culturally and politically.

But of course, as is almost always the case with men and women of singular gifts, 'singular' proves to be the least appropriate of adjectives. It is no surprise to find that in 1997, marking the choir's 20th anniversary, a major work of his for soloists, chamber choir, full chorus and full orchestra, *Le Testament de Villon*, was given its première at the Salle Pleyel by the Chorus and Orchestre de Paris, conducted by John Nelson; and an arresting composition it proved to be (I have heard a cassette of the performance). So it is not only as chorus master that Oldham claims our attention but also as composer, one moreover with a history of unique interest.

Most people with music as their enthusiasm, whether at home or abroad, know of the existence of the great concert hall at Snape in Suffolk and its association with Benjamin Britten. Perhaps fewer have close knowledge of the Old Mill that is nearby, that was Britten's Suffolk home for a number of years and, most memorably, was where *Peter Grimes* was composed. Fewer people still, I think, will be aware that it was precisely there that the young Oldham, after a meeting with Britten in London (Oldham, like Britten before him, was a student at the Royal College of Music), was invited for the weekends to give some

5

help with an opera Britten was writing: 'it turned out to be *Peter Grimes'*, as Oldham laconically remarks.

His reminiscences of those days are often riveting; for example, this exchange about an orchestration exercise he had completed at the College: 'After looking at my work in silence for some minutes, Britten seized upon one isolated note. Noting that I had scored it for a solo horn he said, "Yes, but had you *not* chosen a horn, what other instrument would be effective?" "A clarinet?", I queried. "That would be the obvious answer", he replied, "but what about a double-bass playing very high?" This highly unorthodox solution delighted me. . .' The story in fact continues, both illuminatingly and entertainingly, and I am not going to spoil the reader's enjoyment by anticipating its dénouement. But it is typical of these recollections generated by an extraordinarily formative and productive relationship between Britten and his impressionable part-time assistant and pupil.

The relationship was to develop; and we can read and be reminded of the prominent role Oldham was to play in the very early years of the Aldeburgh Festival and the later evolution of the English Opera Group. In 1952 (the year of the Fifth Festival) *Love in a Village*, a ballad opera of 1762 in three acts, in a new musical version by Arthur Oldham, designed by Osbert Lancaster, produced by Basil Coleman and conducted by Norman Del Mar, was given its première. The cast-list speaks – no, sings – for itself; for example, Norman Lumsden, Nancy Evans, Gladys Parr, Peter Pears and April Cantelo, all of them names so closely associated with Aldeburgh, were among the performers; and Basil Coleman has told us that Oldham not only 'harmonised and scored the original airs for the usual English Opera Group orchestra' but added 'a prelude for harp'.

There is of course more, much more, to read and reflect on, and as I have already suggested there were many years and many activities located in places other than Aldeburgh. There is furthermore a life story told which is by no means free of tragedy and turbulence and challenges, some of which few of us would have had the strength to survive. But as Arthur Oldham would, I believe, be the first to recognise, Music has enabled him to round off an extraordinarily rich and diverse life, to

6

achieve happiness and serenity – he now lives with his wife deep in rural France when not working in Paris – and to write this vivid memoir, which will surely encourage many others to explore and assess the contribution that he has made to musical life in the second half of the century just passed.

Donald Mitchell

London, May 2000

For Annie

# I – Early Years (1926 – 1943)

My father was 62 years old when I was born and, since he died 12 years later, I only ever knew him as an elderly, rather withdrawn, gentleman much given to muttering rather testily to himself as he took me by the hand for long walks in the local park. He had not worked regularly since he lost his job as a journalist at the time of the Great Depression in the early 1930s and had no doubt withdrawn into his own private world of memories of better days spent with his literary and musical colleagues at the turn of the century (he was almost 40 when Queen Victoria died). Prior to the Great War, he was actively participating in the cultural life of his country, contributing articles on politics and religion to the more erudite journals of the day. A staunch monarchist, he would invariably stand rigidly to attention whenever the National Anthem was being played on the radio, and his political preferences were markedly Conservative. I remember him once dismissing Lloyd George as 'a jumped-up little Welshman – all blow and hair'. Although his hands were crippled with rheumatism at the time I knew him, I subsequently learned that he had been an accomplished pianist with a penchant for the works of Chopin.

My mother, on the other hand, was his complete antithesis. Of Dutch descent – she used frequently to boast that her father had emigrated from Haarlem to become pastry-cook to Queen Victoria – she was of an extravert, almost brash, disposition whose chief claim to musical competence was her ability to play the whole of Mendelssohn's *Spring Song* without ever lifting her right foot from the sustaining pedal. But she exuded warmth and love and managed, on a tiny income, to keep her family well fed and clothed and even, on occasions, to provide little treats for my sister and me, such as visits to the seaside and expeditions to the country or to the local cinema.

The relationship between two such contrasted characters was inevitably strained and latterly deteriorated into a war of silence punctuated by the occasional outburst of violence. I remember being puzzled, in a fairly objective way, by how it was that, after chasing my father up the stairs with a large carving knife, my mother succeeded in doing him less damage than when, on a previous occasion, she had pursued him with a pencil as her only weapon.

But, all in all, I consider that I had a very happy childhood. I adored each of my parents as individuals and could never understand why two such nice people could fail to live happily together.

My mother encouraged me to work hard at the local primary school and kept her promise to me to buy me my first bicycle when, at the age of ten, I eventually won a scholarship to the local County Grammar School.

By this time I had already discovered music or, rather, had been made aware of its existence by a sympathetic schoolteacher who had singled me out to sing solos to my class and who would accompany me on the piano. It would appear that I was blessed with a singularly beautiful soprano voice and an aptitude for learning songs very rapidly. My mother transferred me from our tiny mission church, where my principal occupation had been to hand-pump the rather primitive organ, to a more grandiose establishment which boasted its own choir of men and boys and where I rapidly rose to the dizzy heights of principal soprano soloist, performing such standard repertorial masterpieces as *Hear my Prayer* and *Oh, for the Wings of a Dove* for the edification of many a tearful matron in the packed congregation. It is perhaps interesting to record at this point that my fame as a boy singer reached such proportions that the authorities of Southwark Cathedral Choir School proposed, as a reward for my musical contribution, that I should be given a complete education with a view to an eventual career in music. My mother refused the offer on the grounds that music was an 'unsafe' profession and that, in any case, she had earmarked me as a future Civil Servant in the Customs and Excise division. She never told me of the incident, and I only learned about it some 50 years later in a chance conversation with my sister.

Parallel to my singing I was also teaching myself to play the piano. My sister had had a few lessons very early on but had quickly abandoned them under the influence of a very bad teacher who rapped her fingers with a wooden ruler each time she played a wrong note.

Logic dictated that if one child was unsuited to the piano, the other would be also. So I was left to my own devices and would spend hours alone, puzzling through the piles of scores at my disposal until I could relate what was on the printed page to what my fingers where doing on the keyboard. It was not until I was 11 years old that a very competent amateur pianist, who happened also to be a member of my church choir, offered to give me free lessons, arguing that 'this boy is clearly so gifted musically that, when his voice breaks, he will suffer a great loss in his life'. This was the first of many kindnesses from which I have benefited throughout my musical career. When this same teacher was eventually called up to serve in the armed forces during the Second World War, his place was ably taken by the music teacher at my grammar school, who also continued to teach me without asking any fee.

My happy childhood came to an abrupt end with the death of my father, followed two years later, when I was 14 years old, by the suicide of my mother. For many years life had become increasingly burdensome to her. We had moved to a small café-cum-restaurant where she, an excellent cook, managed to eke out a meagre existence to support all of us by dint of an immense amount of hard work and creative economising. This regime, made even more difficult by the exigencies of rationing in the early days of the war, eventually took its toll. She became depressed and began drinking heavily. On her last evening she told me that she intended to take her life by means of the gas oven. She tried to extract from me a promise that I would never become a musician, but that I would pursue her plans for me to become a Civil Servant. It was an assurance I was unable to give her since I had long ago decided that music, in some form or another, was to become my whole life. Due to our straitened circumstances I was still, at the age of 14, obliged to share a bed with my mother, and I resolved that night to save her life by remaining awake and coming downstairs to switch off the gas before it was too late. The inevitable happened. I fell asleep and upon waking, and finding myself alone in bed, crept downstairs, only to discover that I had slept too long. If these details seem gruesome, I feel it is necessary to recount then in order to explain the turbulence which dominated my own personal life from that moment on. I held myself responsible for my mother's death.

Shortly afterwards the family broke up. My elder half-sister (my father's daughter by a previous marriage) took a small apartment where she was able to provide a roof for my sister but not for me. I was accordingly farmed out to a family in the parish and interviewed at regular intervals by a lady social worker. This family, although kind to me, was hardly able to provide the best environment for a budding musician. To begin with they were all, mother, father and two sons, completely tone-deaf, whilst at the same being enthusiastic amateur pianists. I would listen in amazement as they picked out popular melodies with their right hands whilst accompanying them with totally irrelevant harmonies played by their left hand – often singing as they did so. Being by this time a very insecure and aggressive young man, I took great pains to point out to them the errors of their ways. This, as can be imagined, did little to increase my popularity and, sensing this without really understanding the cause, I took to spending all my evenings at the local parish church trying desperately to come to grips with the complexities of the Grieg Piano Concerto on a small upright piano until darkness fell and I was able to return to my bed with a minimum of contact with my adoptive family.

As this point I feel I should introduce another person for whose humanity and kindness I shall always remain grateful. It was an accepted part of school discipline that any pupil whose misconduct merited severe punishment would be obliged to remain at school for an hour on a Friday evening instead of being allowed to go home with his companions. If such a 'detention', as it was called, occurred more than six times in a term, the offending pupil was summoned to the headmaster's office, where he would be invited to 'bend over and admire my carpet, boy' and duly beaten over the bottom with a bamboo cane. Although a thoroughly disruptive pupil who qualified for this ultimate sanction on many occasions, I was never beaten. As an alternative to writing out lists of Latin verbs during my detention periods, my headmaster would order me to go into the school hall, where there was a fine piano, and to 'compose a piece of music' which was to be presented to him the following day. He also expected me to report to his office each Monday morning to receive a small sum of money from his own pocket in order that I should not feel at a disadvantage in relation to my fellow pupils. I do not think he ever told anybody about this.

During my 15th year there occurred two events which had a considerable impact on my future life. The first was a performance which I heard on the radio of the Liszt B minor Sonata. I simply could not believe that only one pair of hands could be capable of playing so many notes at the same time, and I was forced to the unpalatable conclusion that I had begun studying the piano far too late ever to make my living as a concert pianist. The second event concerned a visit to a Promenade Concert, at the invitation of my history teacher, where I was able to witness, for the first time, a full symphony orchestra in all its glory.

Shortly after these two defining experiences I abandoned the family with whom I had been living and spent the whole of my time at school composing great choral and orchestral masterpieces, long since relegated to merciful oblivion, and sleeping, with my kind headmaster's permission, on a mattress in a small store-room. Approaching my 16th year my music teacher submitted a selection of my works to the director of the Royal College of Music in London, who duly awarded me a composition scholarship. This was accompanied by a further small grant from my local authority which enabled me to live while I studied.

# II – The Royal College of Music
## (1943 – 1945)

Mornings on the steps of the Royal College of Music. A small band of enthusiasts waiting for the doors to open at nine o'clock in order to rush in and grab the best practice rooms before the professors arrived to begin their lessons. A new and wonderful world where *everybody* is a musician and where one is no longer the strange and rather isolated exception in remote suburban Surrey.

The students could be divided into roughly three categories: those of us who were there by means of a scholarship (the keenest, perhaps the most gifted, but certainly those most determined to make the best of their time and to succeed), the paying students, and a small group of well-bred young ladies whose affluent parents had sent them there to be 'finished' since, due to the war, the Sorbonne and Switzerland were no longer available.

The standard of teaching varied widely. The then director of the college, Sir George Dyson, a competent if not very distinguished composer (*The Canterbury Pilgrims* is his best-known work), was initially kind and encouraging. Aware of my family background, he offered either to pay for all of my music or to give me an extra study. I chose the latter alternative and, on his advice, opted to learn the organ. It was a mistake. After a year of solid Stanford *Preludes and Postludes* with a very dull teacher I was eventually allowed to begin studying some Bach. But it was too late. By this time I had come to loathe the organ as an instrument ('the monster that never breathes' as Stravinsky succinctly put it) and I abandoned it in favour of learning the timpani. This was a much happier choice and led to my becoming the regular timpanist in the college orchestra and thus being able to participate in corporate music-making and to acquiring a knowledge of the standard orchestral repertoire.

My piano teacher, Kathleen Long, was a patient and dedicated soul who, in spite of my late start, managed to bring me to a level where

I was able to accompany competently and even to be chosen to play my first concerto (Beethoven No 1) at one of the regular college concerts.

As composition teacher, I was allotted Herbert Howells, a rather vain little man who would constantly refer me to his own works as an example of how music should be written. Some of his advice seems, in retrospect, to have been quite remarkable in its ineptitude. 'Never study the works of Rimsky-Korsakov if you wish to learn how to orchestrate', he told me, 'otherwise you will only end up orchestrating like him'.

During my first year I was writing copious amounts of music of all kinds, most of which was never seriously looked at by Howells, he being frequently engaged in long conversations with his prettier female students during my study periods. It was clearly a most unsatisfactory situation from my point of view and I continued to plough a lone furrow, composing pieces which I would perform, for our own amusement, with my fellow students. One of these works, a quintet for contralto voice and strings, was performed at a college chamber music concert. The following night the director of the college participated in a radio programme during which he roundly condemned my piece as being 'cacophonous' and 'self-consciously modern'. He was probably right, but I found it a curious attitude for him to adopt towards one of his own students, although the notoriety it gave me was more encouraging than otherwise.

The year concluded nevertheless on a positive note. I was awarded the Grade IV composition prize and also the Cobbett Prize for chamber music, the two together bringing in some very welcome pocket money.

It is worth mentioning, in view of subsequent events, that I volunteered for the Navy at this time; less, I have to admit, out of patriotism than out of a desire to profit from the six months at Cambridge University which would have led to a commission. This was the year 1943 and my application was viewed by all and sundry as a proof that I was a good fellow with a right sense of his priorities. I failed to pass my medical examination, due to poor eyesight, and my life as a student continued.

Included in one of the college concerts, in which I participated as timpanist, was a work by Britten: *Rejoice in the Lamb*. I listened to it awestruck. It seem to encapsulate everything that I believed in in composition: inventiveness, charm, a mastery of technique and a real professionalism. At the conclusion of the concert I hurried round to introduce myself to the composer and handed him some of my songs, which he promised to look at. Three months passed, but I heard nothing. Noting that Britten was scheduled to give a recital with Peter Pears at the Wigmore Hall, I bought myself a seat and, once again, presented myself. 'Have you had a chance to look at my songs?' I asked Britten. He replied that he had, that he liked them very much, and that he intended to include one of them in his next recital with Pears. 'Will you accept me as a pupil?' He told me that this presented problems since he did not take pupils. There was a further inconvenience in that he spent most of his time in Suffolk, while I was based in London. 'However', he said, 'if you would care to come down to Suffolk and spend some of your weekends with me, I could use some help with an opera I am writing (it turned out to be *Peter Grimes*) and we could at the same time talk about music in general and I could look at what you have been writing'. 'Composition can't be taught', he added, 'you either have the gift or you haven't; but by working with a composer, quite a lot can rub off which could be useful to you'. It was his very modest way of introducing me to a world which rapidly became of paramount importance to my musical development and it was an opportunity which filled me with joy.

My second year at the college meant that, of necessity, I was leading a double life. Ostensibly I was continuing to be a model student, taking a full and very active part in curricular activities, whilst spending most of my weekends with Britten at the Old Mill in Snape. Thus I had not one but two composition teachers and this led to some curious and amusing situations. One of the exercises which Howells had set me was to orchestrate the first movement of a Beethoven piano sonata. Before submitting my efforts to Howells, I first showed them to Britten for his comments. After looking at my work in silence for some minutes he seized upon one isolated note. Noting that I had scored it for a solo horn he said 'Yes; but had you *not* chosen a horn, what other instrument would be effective?' 'A clarinet?' I queried. 'That would be the obvious answer', he replied, 'but what about a solo double-bass playing very high?'. This highly unorthodox solution delighted me but nevertheless I left my manuscript as it was and in due course took it along to Howells. By an extraordinary coincidence he seized upon precisely the same note as Britten and posed exactly the same question. 'Had you not scored this for a horn, what *could* it have been?' Emboldened by the counsel I had secretly received from Britten, I replied 'A double-bass playing very high'. 'Nonsense', said Howells, '... a clarinet'. I think this little incident sheds much light upon the academic approach of Howells in contrast to the thoughtful, original attitude to composition which was unique to Britten. Many times he would stress the importance of searching, even painfully, for the *right* solution to a problem rather than accepting the first one which came to mind (usually dictated by what the current text-books had laid down). 'It is better', he would say, 'to spend three weeks writing one good song than to write six indifferent ones in the same period'. Later, he was to contradict his own dictum when discussing Tippett's first opera, *A Midsummer Marriage*. 'Michael takes *so long* to write an opera', he complained. 'It would have been better if he had written three operas in the same period of time because he would have learned more about stagecraft'. Both points of view contain a certain logic, although it worth recording that Tippett was unqualified in his admiration of Britten as a composer. 'Ben writes music as easily as the rest of us breathe air', he once told me.

Meanwhile, life as a student was continuing happily. As the now confirmed percussionist with the college orchestra it fell to me to participate in a wide variety of concerts and operatic productions. The latter came to an abrupt end due partly to my over-exuberance, and partly to a rather wicked sense of humour which I felt unable to contain. At a rehearsal of Mendelssohn's incidental music to *A Midsummer Night's Dream* I managed to search out from the instrument chest the largest pair of cymbals I had ever seen. At the opening tutti chord of the *Wedding March* I clashed them so loudly that the rehearsal had to be abandoned for five minutes while my instrumental colleagues recovered from temporary deafness. On another occasion I was designated to play the cuckoo in a production of *Hansel and Gretel*. This curious instrument consisted of two flat pieces of wood, hinged in the middle, and with a small set of bellows at either end. If you pressed one end it said 'Cuc' and if you pressed the other end it said 'Koo'. Naturally I could not resist pressing the ends in the wrong order, which made the poor bird sing his song in inversion ('Koo-cuc') and I was duly relieved of my post as the official Royal College of Music cuckoo-player.

It was at about this time that I received my first commission as a composer. I was asked by the Ballet Rambert to write the score for a ballet to be entitled *Mr Punch*. I set about the task happily and with great pride and in due course the ballet was successfully performed ('... the English *Petrouchka*...' said one critic. What exaggerated rubbish!) and it was incorporated into the repertoire of the company. I submitted parts of the score, together with other pieces, to the college authorities for consideration when awarding the end-of-the-year composition prizes. So confident was I of winning the money that I spent it in advance. Very pointedly, and to my intense chagrin, no composition prizes were awarded that year. Let me explain what happened.

Following the very successful première of *Peter Grimes*, Britten had written the incidental music to a play by Ronald Duncan (later his librettist for *The Rape of Lucretia*) entitled *This Way to the Tomb*. The music was scored for a small *a cappella* choir, piano duet, and jazz percussion, and was produced on a shoe-string budget at the tiny Mercury Theatre in Notting Hill Gate.

Initially scheduled for a very limited period, the verse-play, or *Masque and Anti-Masque* as Duncan chose to call it, achieved an almost immediate triumph, helped considerably by the brilliant performance of Robert Speaight in the rôle of St Anthony, and was eventually transferred to London's West End. Britten's incidental music played no small part in this success, and to the three songs which he had written for one of St Anthony's companions he added, during the course of preparatory rehearsals, an exquisite fragment for solo soprano to be sung off-stage. He sent this to me, together with a covering note (see illustration section). It is interesting to note that the first three musical intervals of this fragment are identical, even to the key in which they are written, to the opening notes of the first of the *Sea Interludes* from *Peter Grimes*. Ben, clearly being pushed by Duncan for this additional fragment, quickly produced what was needed by making use of material still fresh in his mind (both the *Tomb* and *Grimes* received their premières in 1945).

Britten had asked me to form a choir from my fellow-students to sing the *a cappella* portions and to find a couple of pianists to play the duets. I, naturally, became the jazz percussionist and was placed in overall charge of the music. One of the pianists was my bosom friend John Lindsay, also a scholar. In due course the college authorities came to hear of our appointments and we were officially informed that we could either continue to be full-time students or part-time professionals, but not both at the same time. This ridiculous policy, now, I believe, abandoned, meant that young instrumentalists were effectively barred from having any contact with the world of professional music-making, with the result that many suffered prolonged periods of unemployment when their student days came to on end.

Lindsay and I took our problem to Britten, who, with typical pragmatism, said 'Well, you'll have to start your professional careers some time, so why not now?'. We accepted his advice and abandoned our scholarships. This left the problem of finding a piano teacher for my friend to continue his studies privately. With great generosity, again typical of the man, Britten found a fine teacher for Lindsay and paid for the lessons out his own pocket.

# III – Working With Britten (1944 – 1952)

My visits to the Old Mill at Snape soon began to take on a regular pattern. Sometimes Ben and I would meet in London and travel down to Suffolk together on the train. There was not much opportunity for conversation on these journeys since Ben was usually occupied in correcting proofs of his most recent compositions or in preparing schemes for new ones. On other occasions I would travel down alone and Ben would meet me at Saxmundham station in a modest open-topped sports car and drive me to the Old Mill to begin what rapidly became our daily routine. Ben's 'workshop' was situated on the first floor of the mill tower. He would sit at a large table on one side of the room, scoring his opera *Peter Grimes* at what seemed to me to be an incredible rate, while I would have another table at the other side of the room, where I would prepare the next pages of manuscript for him by writing in the clefs and key-signatures and ruling the bar-lines. Usually he would explain to me what he was working on. I remember him telling me that he was short of words for the great choral fugue 'Old Joe has gone fishing' and we had a lot of fun inventing new verses and rhymes together, some of which, I believe, eventually found their way into the final version. In no way do I wish to take credit for these minute contributions, if such they were. It was merely Ben's way of involving me in a practical way in what he himself was doing and thus relieving me to a certain extent of what could otherwise have become a rather monotonous task.

Lunch was prepared by his sister Beth and afterwards we would go for long walks over the Suffolk marshes and simply talk about life and about music. I remember once discussing the question of honours with him (I think it was about the time that Winston Churchill had accepted a knighthood). He told me that he would prefer to wait until he was offered a peerage and added, jokingly, 'Then I can become Lord Britten of Snape!' I also recall a conversation we had about the art of accompaniment: 'There are only two categories of musician who really understand it: composers and Gerald Moore.' I rapidly learned that his favourite composers were Mozart (of course!), Verdi, Tchaikovsky,

Chopin, etc. He also had a profound admiration for Stravinsky and introduced me to his *Symphony of Psalms*, written barely fifteen years previously. I confessed to a similar admiration for this brilliant composer and told Ben that my ultimate dream was to go America to study with him. With a wry smile he said 'Why don't you stick around here a bit longer? You may not then find it necessary...'. Unfortunately this great admiration, almost reverence, that Britten felt towards Stravinsky was to have an unhappy apotheosis many years later when, with Ben at the height of his powers and his place in the hierarchy of 20th-century composers firmly established, whilst the reputation and output of Stravinsky were on the decline, there appeared an article in a well-known periodical in which Stravinsky was asked for his opinion of the younger composer's *War Requiem*. He was alleged to have replied 'Britten's music is like Kleenex, you use it once and then throw it away'. Ben got to hear of the remark and was deeply wounded by it. From then on he began to be severely critical of Stravinsky's music. When I praised the brilliant orchestration of *Petrouchka* he replied that it did not sound as if it had been originally conceived for the instruments, only '...like a grand piano orchestrated'.

After a further late-afternoon period of work, we would light the paraffin lamps (Snape, at that time, possessed no electricity supply), have an early dinner and settle down to listen to music on a primitive gramophone. I remember Ben being particularly proud of the first-ever recording of his *Serenade* for tenor, horn, and strings (with Pears, Dennis Brain and the Boyd Neel Orchestra and still, to my mind, the best recording of the work ever made).

He would also find time to look at what I had been writing, to discuss it with me (he never 'criticised', but only made suggestions) and to set me exercises which he thought would be helpful to me: the first being, I recall, to write a Mass in the style of Palestrina. Unlike Howells, he never ever referred me to his own compositions as examples but would point me rather in the direction of particular composers from whom he felt I could learn. I recently came across a copy of a letter I wrote to my friend John Lindsay in April 1948. It presents, I feel, a vivid picture of the relationship existing between Ben and me at that time:

My dear John, . . . , An awful lot's been happening lately. My session with Ben tonight was the most wonderful one I've ever had. I had tea with him, and then we went into the studio (on our own all the time) and began to talk about Variations in general – and my piece (*Variations on a Carol Tune*) in particular. For the first time I was able to talk easily to him, on the same level. He wasn't tired, or pressed for time; everything was perfect. He asked me to describe what I'd done, and my plans for the piece, in detail and then asked me to play them. And (again for the first time and to my intense delight) I was able to play them calmly, and just as I do to you; pointing out the good bits as I went along, and with Ben agreeing and looking as pleased as me with a right chord. He likes what I've done very much; and made some excellent suggestions which I agree with completely. He wants the Theme lengthened by repetitions because the later Variations are longer and complete pieces in themselves. Then he played me the Mozart Variations on *Ah je dirai vous, Maman* with great poetry and intelligence. He asked me if I had a score of *The Young Person's Guide* and, because I hadn't, gave me one 'with my love'. All the time [we] were talking and I told him how highly I rated his work – that I thought 'On the First of May' (the concerted item in the first scene of *Herring*) was on a par with the Mozart operas. He at once said that he could never believe that himself and gave me his reasons: all of which were perfectly honest. He rates his work well below Mozart's; but said how terribly happy it made him to hear such a thing said about his work by a person 'of such tremendously promising gifts and very great sensitivity'. I convinced him I really *did* believe what I had said; and it also pleased him because he himself feels there is nothing at all in the particular piece of which to be ashamed and he felt it was a promising sign that I had singled it out.

Don't get the idea that this was a mutual admiration society! Not at all; it was just a completely honest talk which has given me enormous personal help and confidence. Ben says that from now on I will find it easier to compose – because I know more of what I'm doing – although he warned me of some very gloomy days that are bound to come always. They did to Mozart and they do to him. Just before I went he asked if he could play *me* (!!!) his new Scena from *The Beggar's Opera*; which is very wonderful (it's the one ending with *Greensleeves*). I found out something he dislikes (which I'd suspected all along). He hates apologies. At one point I apologised for my ignorance over some detail in the Variations and he at once made it plain that one *shouldn't* apologise for things. Altogether I was with him for about two hours.

Oh yes! He asked me how I felt, hearing my piece at Saturday's concert. I told him I loathed every minute of it; and he said *he* does too, with his own pieces – 'That's why I can never bear to go and see *Grimes*.'

So [I] feel a lot better. Actually I think I was blaming his playing for a good deal of my own peculiar frame of mind at the time. It's a long time since

I wrote the Donne – and there's been much better stuff since – and I hated it and thought everyone else did too. But Ben assured me that, if he and Peter hadn't thought very highly of it, they would never have done it!

His attitude to composition was, as I have already indicated, that it could not be taught. He would cite the example of Renaissance painters and sculptors who would gradually learn their craft by working in a humble capacity with established masters. They would begin by learning to mix clay and paint, graduate over the years to helping their masters complete their works, and only then begin to produce unaided originals. In a similar way he taught me simple rules for preparing manuscript scores. 'Try, wherever possible', he told me, 'to make your bars of equal length, however many notes they contain, because this makes the music easier to read'. He also showed me how to erase an error in the manuscript by first scratching out the offending note with a razor blade, then rubbing the surface with a hard bone pen-holder, and finally putting in the correct note by using the back of the pen-nib. These may seem insignificant details, but they were to become of immense practical use to me later on. They were, if you like, Ben's equivalent of the Renaissance pupils learning to mix clay, and they illustrate his whole attitude to composition: at once extremely professional and also practical.

Being aware that, with my scholarship now gone and having virtually no money upon which to survive, he arranged a contract for me with his publishers, Boosey and Hawkes, whereby I would receive a small sum each month 'in advance of future royalties' and introduced me to Erwin Stein, himself a distinguished musician and a former pupil of Schoenberg, at that time in charge of proof-reading at Boosey and Hawkes. I was paid one penny per page for correcting proofs of soon-to-be-published compositions, and would sit up far into the night in order to earn small sums of money. Stein proved to be not only the ultimate perfectionist but also a very hard task-master. Frequently he would scan several pages of my carefully corrected proofs before seizing upon one missed staccato and proclaiming triumphantly '…and what about *this*, my dear?' It could have been soul-destroying work but was not, since I had the opportunity to study all the works of Stravinsky which were being re-edited at that time (1947), and also masterpieces such at the

*Concerto for Orchestra* of Bartók. Bartók's genius was, at that time, recognised by a relative minority of practising musicians, and his works only became world-famous a few years later, after his death in comparative poverty.

Four years had now elapsed since I had begun my studies with Britten. Having secured for me a certain minimal financial security, with the contract at Boosey and Hawkes, he now began actively to encourage my work by helping me to obtain commissions and performances. The first of these was a piece for tenor and string orchestra, consisting of settings of Shakespeare sonnets, and which I had entitled *Summer's Lease*.

Realising that I would need peace and domestic equilibrium in order to write the piece, Ben very kindly arranged with one of his Suffolk neighbours, Norah Nichols, widow of the poet Robert Nichols, to stay at her house for a month, during which I completed my composition. Norah was a kind and discreet hostess, well accustomed to existing alongside the artistic temperament, and our friendship matured and blossomed. I was to use her home as a base for composing for the next six years.

*Summer's Lease* duly received its première at Chelsea Town Hall, with Peter Pears as soloist and with myself conducting the Boyd Neel String Orchestra. Ben was critical: perhaps, I suspect, because it was a rather blatant attempt on my part to rival the success of his own *Seven Sonnets of Michelangelo*, which had recently been published.

My own chief recollection of the concert was arriving at Chelsea Town Hall having forgotten my trousers. I rushed home in a taxi and got back only just in time to pick up my baton. The incident, of course, caused much hilarity and resulted in more press attention than the actual music. Ben, in spite of being disappointed with the piece, continued to encourage me and promptly invited me to compose a work for his first Aldeburgh Festival (1948).

The work I submitted was *Variations on a Carol Tune** and Ben was of considerable help to me with advice on scoring for a chamber orchestra: my previous compositions, mostly ballets (see Chapter IV), having been conceived for larger ensembles. I recall him examining the score and suggesting that one extended solo, which I had given to an oboe in a rather low register, would sound much better on a cor anglais. He was, of course, right, and I amended the score accordingly.

The piece was received politely by the public, but savaged by the critics. One has to remember that at that time dissonance still retained its ability to shock (although my kind of dissonance was mild by today's standards) and, in this sense, I was considered something of a revolutionary. The critic of the *East Anglian Times* described my variations as 'a beautiful tune crushed by a steam-roller'. Ben sought to re-assure me by advising me to ignore such remarks (he had even tried to hide the notice to prevent me seeing it and was quite angry when somebody showed it to me). He himself was, of course, extremely sensitive to adverse criticism, of which he himself had received plenty. But he always managed to overcome his initial anger and to move on to the next project. In so doing the bad period was, if not entirely forgotten, at least put into proportion. This philosophy he was clearly attempting to pass on to me.

While still a student at the Royal College of Music, I had composed three songs to translations of Chinese texts. During a brief tour in Paris, where *This Way to the Tomb* was performed at the Studio des Champs Elysées, I included these in a recital which I gave at the home of Lady Duff Cooper, whose husband was at that time British Ambassador. Ben and Peter got to hear of them and suggested that I should expand the group. With two new additions, they included my *Five Chinese Lyrics* in a recital of English songs, the concluding concert of the 1949 Aldeburgh Festival. They were an immediate success, were recorded (three of them) by Britten and Pears, and remain in the repertoire to this day.

---

* see page 22

In 1951 a second cycle of songs followed, which I entitled *The Commandment of Love*. This comprised settings of six poems by the 14th-century mystical poet Richard Rolle of Hampole. Apart from the fourth item, *My Song is in Sighing*, which Ben greatly admired (he described it as 'a real contribution') when he played the cycle through with me at Norah Nichols's house, these were unmemorable. Ben and Peter duly gave them a hearing at the Festival and they were then published. In spite of a few subsequent performances, however, they never achieved the success or popularity of the *Chinese Lyrics*. (Interestingly, Ben subsequently had success with his own settings of Chinese lyrics for tenor and guitar, *Songs from the Chinese*.)

The following year Ben asked me to contribute an opera to the Aldeburgh Festival. A year or so previously, he had made a very successful 'realisation' of the celebrated *The Beggar's Opera*, an opus which has intrigued men of the theatre from John Gay, in 1728, to Kurt Weill (*Die Dreigroschenoper*) in the 1930s, and even to the present day. This word 'realisation' needs, perhaps, a word of explanation. In its strict sense it implies a given melodic line, together with a figured bass, the latter being then filled out, or 'realised', to provide a complete accompaniment. Britten had adopted a much looser interpretation, retaining only the melodies, which he then used as a basis for an entirely fresh composition: new harmonies, contrapuntal textures, etc. It was in this spirit that he proposed to me to compose *Love in a Village* for his English Opera Group. Peter Pears, one of whose hobbies was browsing in second-hand bookshops, had discovered an 18th-century volume which contained Dr Arne's original version of this so-called 'ballad opera'. Britten had, by this time, encapsulated an orchestral formula consisting of only 12 players (five solo strings, four woodwind, horn harp, and percussion), which was viable for touring purposes. It was proposed that I should orchestrate accordingly. Frank Howes, at that time critic of *The Times* newspaper, wrote an article commending Britten's brilliance at being able to work within these orchestral limits, but gave it as his opinion that such a formula could only succeed for someone of Britten's genius. With all the arrogance of youth, I replied to Howes's article, pointing out that, 'as the next composer of an opera for the English Opera Group, I would take pains to prove him [Howes] wrong'. The letter duly appeared (the one and only time I have ever written to *The Times*) and elicited a warm and encouraging reply from Lord Harewood, at that time a close friend and fervent admirer of Britten.

*Love in a Village* was produced by Basil Coleman with a distinguished cast, including Peter Pears, Norman Lumsden, Nancy Evans and Heddle Nash, was well received at the Aldeburgh Festival, and remained in the repertoire of the English Opera Group for several subsequent seasons.

1952 was a particularly onerous year for me. I had not wished to accept the proposed commission from the BBC to write *Love in a Village*. But, rather than turn it down (it had, after all, been organised for me by Ben), I decided to ask for what I considered to be an exorbitant fee, half of which was to be paid in advance, hoping that my conditions would be considered sufficiently outrageous to annihilate the project. To my consternation a contract arrived, by return of post, together with a cheque for 50 per cent of my asking fee. I was committed. But it meant that I had somehow, within the space of three short months, to write my song-cycle for Britten and Pears, my opera *Love in a Village*, and a ballet for Covent Garden.

In spite of increasing stress and mental fatigue, occasioned by anxiety to meet deadlines, I did manage to make one minor contribution to the 1953 Aldeburgh Festival. Ben invited me, together with five well-known composers (Tippett, Berkeley, himself, Searle and Walton) to submit a variation on a theme, by Byrd, of *Sellenger's Round*. I honestly cannot remember ever having heard the piece, although I continue to this day to receive royalties from it, and I suspect that my contribution was the least distinguished. My mind was tired and my confidence was flagging. It was not helped by an incident, which I now see as amusing, connected with the first performance. For this occasion the names of the composers were announced, but not connected to any particular variation. The audience was invited, for a small prize, to link the composers to their own variations. I asked John Amis, the distinguished critic and broadcaster, whether he had succeeded in solving the puzzle. 'No problem at all.' he replied. 'Even *my* variation?' I queried, feeling rather flattered. 'Oh, yours was the easiest of all.' he said. 'The other five were so clearly identifiable by their individual styles that that only left you!'

Much has been written and said about Britten's tendency to make use of people and then to suddenly drop them when they no longer served his purpose, often leaving them resentful and hurt. I had made the vocal scores of *The Beggar's Opera*, *The Little Sweep*, and the *Spring Symphony*, and the fact that my name ceased to appear as a regular contributor to the Aldeburgh Festival after 1953, has led to speculation about whether this was not so in my case. I am happy that this book gives me the opportunity to refute any such suggestions, and to be able to explain precisely what happened.

A year before the now well-documented cruise up the Rhine in 1951, in which I, together with Basil Coleman and a few fishermen from Aldeburgh, were guests of Pears and Britten, I had gone to Basle in Switzerland for the première of my ballet *Circus Canteen*. There I had begun a torrid relationship with Nicole Breton, the prima ballerina who had danced the leading rôle in my piece. This relationship was still ongoing in 1951, and I had made it quite clear to Ben and Peter, before the voyage started from Aldeburgh, that I intended to leave the party when we reached our furthest point south (it happened to be Koblenz), in order to continue my journey by train to Basle. This news was not particularly well received, especially by Peter, although I was nevertheless taken along in spite of a certain frostiness evident in the atmosphere as we set off. This was not helped by the fact that, as soon as we made landfall in Holland, most of the crew, together with myself, made a beeline for the local hostelries and got very drunk. Peter Pears had decreed, unwisely in my opinion, that there was to be no alcohol carried aboard, with the inevitable result that resentment built up among the crew. 'This is a right dry old ship,' remarked Billy Burrell wryly as we made our way across the North Sea. Humphrey Carpenter, in his biography of Britten, quotes me as saying that 'it was on the whole a sober and serious journey'. On the whole. But for me it was not a happy one, and I have to say that I was relieved when I eventually left the ship at Koblenz.

But a further incident, far more serious, was to temporarily sour my relationship with Ben, and for this I must bear the sole responsibility.

By 1954 I had left Norah Nichols and set up home with Nicole in Lodsworth, a small village near Petworth in Sussex. Finding composition harder and harder, and struggling to make ends meet by seeking out commissions to write incidental music for BBC feature programmes (including my one and only collaboration with Louis McNeice), I rang up John Maud (later Sir John) to ask him for money. Maud, at that time a high-ranking civil servant, had been for many years a close associate and admirer of Britten and his music. My request was refused, and Maud informed Britten what I had done. Ben was, justifiably, furious, and lost no time in telling me so. There followed a long period of silence between us. But in no way can Ben be said to have 'dropped' me. I 'dropped' myself.

I think it is greatly to Ben's credit that following the years of my nervous breakdown – the 'Twilight Years' (see Chapter V) – he gradually resumed his musical collaboration with me. In 1965 I accepted a commission from the BBC Transcription Service to write a short *a cappella* piece for that year's Aldeburgh Festival. *St Francis: Blind Audley's Carol* was performed and recorded by Louis Halsey's splendid Elizabethan Singers and was to be my final contribution to Aldeburgh.

By 1968 I was well established in my new career as choral director, and in that year Peter Diamand decided that Britten was to be the featured composer at the Edinburgh Festival. My chorus participated in three of his compositions: *Voices for Today* (a lovely piece, written to commemorate the 20th anniversary of the founding of the United Nations, but hampered, in my opinion, by a text, largely compiled by Peter Pears, which read like a *Reader's Digest* of quotes about pacifism), and the *War Requiem*. Ben came to all the later rehearsals and, as we sat side by side in the Usher Hall discussing minutae of the choral writing (I even dared to criticise one or two passages, such as his division of the tenors into three parts at the Sanctus, in which I always give the lower voice to the first basses, and which suggestion he accepted with equanimity), it was as if the bad times had never been. It was clear that my youthful indiscretions had been forgiven.

In 1971 I visited Ben, at the Red House in Suffolk, to discuss the recording he was to make, together with my London Symphony Chorus, of Elgar's *Dream of Gerontius*. I asked him why he had chosen to record this particular work since, when I had been working with him as his pupil, he had expressed considerable distaste for Elgar's music. 'Well, you know,' he told me, 'I've been looking at the score again, and if you strip off all the encrustations which have accumulated over the years (he was no doubt referring to the Barbirolli 'tradition' which had become the norm for performances of *Gerontius*), there is really a very good piece underneath.' And he proceeded to prove his point by making, at the Snape Maltings, what has come to be regarded as the finest and most faithful recording of this great work.

There was even a 'reconciliation' between myself and Peter Pears when, in 1965, I accompanied him in a recital, at the National Gallery of Scotland, which included six of my songs from *Love in a Village* together with my song-cycle *The Commandment of Love*.

Not long before his death, in December 1976, Ben wrote me two final letters (reproduced here for the first time). One was in response to a tribute to him which I had made in the course of a broadcast to celebrate his 60th birthday and in which I had referred to the many happy years spent as his pupil. The other, which demonstrates so clearly his courage in the face of his final illness, still moves me to tears. For over 40 years we had been friends and musical colleagues.

The world now recognises Britten as a genius. I remember him as a lovely man, my mentor, the primordial influence on my musical development.

THE RED HOUSE, ALDEBURGH-ON-SEA, SUFFOLK, IP15 5PZ.

8th January, 1974.

My dear Arthur,

    As you may know I am undergoing a prolonged and
restricting convalescence at the moment; that is why this
letter of thanks *(for your BBC talk)* is so belated, partly typed and partly
in a shaky scribble.  But it comes with my devoted love
and gratitude not only for the kindly and appreciative
things you said about me and our work together, but for
giving up the time to make the broadcast -- I know full-well
what a bore and time waster this can be!  I should like
to tell you how deeply touched I am that you did it, and by
what you said.  *You brought back those Snape days
so clearly.*

        *Much love to all of you,*

                *Ben*


THE RED HOUSE, ALDEBURGH-ON-SEA, SUFFOLK, IP15 5PZ

3rd June, 1974.

My dear Arthur,
    Thank you for writing me such a lovely letter.  It
really did encourage me at what is rather a low time.  I
have been able to do nothing for a year and it doesn't look
much like changing; still, I must be patient, and affection
and appreciation, like your letter contained, was a great help.
Much love to you all, particularly the new 'Miles!'

                *Ben*

---

NB. the new 'Miles' referred to was the author's son Timothy, making his operatic debut
in *The Turn of the Screw.*

Opening page from one the composer's most recent works – *Dos Villancicos de Santa Teresa de Avila*, for soprano, mezzo soprano and piano, 1997.

Right: The author's father c. 1900.

Left: The author's mother.

A1

Left: A family outing in 1928. The author's father, Arthur Oldham, stepsister Muriel, sister Barbara and himself.

Below: The author as a young man.

(Left: Photo courtesy of the Britten-Pears Library, Aldeburgh)

(Right: Photo Douglas Glass, courtesy of the Britten-Pears Library, Aldeburgh)

1949: Peter Pears sings an aria from Britten's *Billy Budd*, in the course of its composition. At the piano is the composer; centre is writer Ronald Duncan, with Arthur Oldham (right).

Arthur Oldham conducting the choir of St Mary's Roman Catholic Cathedral in 1963. (Photo by courtesy of the Edinburgh Festival Society and the Scottish Tourist Board)

Scene from the 1954 production at Sadler's Wells Theatre, London, of *Love in a Village*.
Centre: Heddle Nash (Hawthorn) and Norman Lumsden (Woodcock).
(Photo, Hulton Getty Picture Collection)

The 'extra' fragment Britten wrote for *The Way to the Tomb*.
In his covering letter, Britten said: 'Here is your fragment. I suggest that she sings it as
many times as necessary – quite slowly and remotely – but each time <u>softer</u>. If it
doesn't do – call me.' The words read: 'O proud heart
Take pity on that part of me which lies in you as your own lost heart'.

# IV – Ballet Days and Soho Nights (1945 – 1947)

Following the success of my first ballet, *Mr Punch*, the director of the company, Madame Rambert, invited me to become her musical director. It was a daunting challenge (I was only 19 years old) since it involved conducting the London seasons of her company. I had only conducted an orchestra on one previous occasion: an *ad hoc* group of extremely fine, but tough, professional instrumentalists (Dennis Brain was my horn player) who gave me a very rough ride as I timidly led them through a score of incidental music which I had composed for a radio programme. At one point I asked the clarinettist why he had failed to play his entry. He replied 'Well, if you don't hold your bloody beat up I can't see it, can I?' and resumed reading his newspaper. As I wandered distraught through the corridors of Broadcasting House, during the interval, the leader of the orchestra, Alfredo Campoli, came up to me and put his arm around my shoulder. 'Don't worry, son,' he said, 'I've seen these buggers make Sargent weep!'

Work with the ballet orchestra was less stressful and a good deal more rewarding. The players, for the most part, were outstanding, although I was plagued, as were most conductors at the time, by the deputy system which meant that one was frequently confronted by a different set of players from those with whom one had rehearsed the previous day. Nevertheless, we managed to master a fairly vast repertoire in a relatively short space of time and duly gave many successful performances.

The fact that the orchestra was not large meant that I was obliged to re-orchestrate many standard works, to compensate for the absence of certain instruments. This proved to be a godsend to me as a young composer, since I was able to hear almost immediately the results of my efforts and so to learn the craft of orchestration much more rapidly than I would otherwise have done. I was also commissioned to compose more ballets for the company and these duly entered the repertoire alongside *Giselle*, *Swan Lake* and other classics which Marie

33

Rambert had retained from her days as a dancer with the Diaghilev Company.

Rambert was a difficult woman. She would invariably post herself in the wings at performances and hurl abuse at her young dancers as they came off stage if they had not lived up to her very high standards. Her conductor was not excepted from these tirades and many times I suffered the rough edge of her tongue when my tempi had not been to her liking. But all the time I was learning. In addition to having a difficult nature, Rambert was also extremely mean. Her employees were over-worked and poorly paid (she justified this practice by saying she was 'encouraging young talent'), and I was no exception. She had promised to commission my second ballet, *The Sailor's Return*, for an agreed sum of money. No contract was forthcoming, however, and when the evening of the first performance arrived, I refused to begin conducting the programme until I had one. The result was that the leader of the orchestra conducted the second Act of *Swan Lake* whilst I sat, shivering with apprehension, in my dressing-room. During the interval a signed contract, commissioning my ballet, duly arrived and I proceeded to conduct the first performance. It was my first lesson in professionalism, but it was far from being my last.

In due course this same leader, a fine violinist and a warm human being, became my close friend and confidante. He asked me one day if I was receiving the royalties due to me as composer for the three of my ballets which were now in the company's repertoire. I told him that Madame Rambert was paying me two shillings and sixpence per performance, whereupon he pulled a long face and arranged to take me along to the Performing Right Society. They listened to my story, verified that the facts were true, and promptly enrolled me as a member. Their legal representatives contacted Rambert, informed her of the appropriate rates, and sent her a large bill for all previous performances of my work. She refused to pay. The Society took out an injunction from a Justice of the Peace to prevent her company from leaving for a tour of Australia until she *had* paid and, since the injunction was served prior to the company boarding the boat at Southampton, she finally handed over the money. Although I lost my job as musical director I gained something far more valuable in the long run: my second lesson in professionalism.

In spite of severing my relations with the Rambert Ballet Company I continued to compose for a medium which I had come to enjoy and feel I understood. In 1950 I accepted a commission from the Stadttheater in Basel to compose the music for a one-act ballet entitled *Circus Canteen*, and in 1952 I had the joy of collaborating with the gifted young choreographer John Cranko, and with the celebrated cartoonist Osbert Lancaster, in a work for the Royal Ballet and produced (in 1952) at Covent Garden. Although well received by Londoners (Osbert's sets were particularly acclaimed), the Royal Ballet was unable to maintain my work in this repertoire when it went on tour to the United States the following year since the story had, as its heroine, a young lady missionary in the Salvation Army who gets eaten by a black man whilst pursuing her vocation in Africa – hence the ballet's title: *Bonne Bouche*. Political correctness, especially with regard to anything which could be construed as racism, was already beginning to substitute itself for a sense of humour.

It was at about this time that I began to enlarge my circle of acquaintances to include other young artists, not necessarily musicians, who shared my ideals and, above all, my growing conviction that a great destiny awaited us all once an uncomprehending world had come to its senses. The process had begun when John Lindsay and I, still students at that time, had decided to share a rented apartment overlooking Clapham Common; at that time a rather bourgeois residential area. We kept open house, not only for our cronies from the College, but also for all kinds of itinerant visitors with any sort of vague connection to the arts. Among these was a small group of Italians, one of whom had had a fascinating background. He was a stocky young man, built like a tank, and with enormous hands, whom we knew as 'Pablo'. Originating from Edinburgh, he had been subject to internment as an enemy alien when war broke out in 1939. However, he was offered an alternative, which was to enrol in the Pioneer Corps of the British Army. He promptly accepted and, equally promptly, regretted his decision. The work was arduous and laborious and consisted of manual labour: digging ditches, building roads and airfields. The Pioneer Corps was universally considered to be the lowest echelon of service in the army, available only to those considered unfit for any other duties. Pablo, unable to escape by any legal means, began to devise a plan whereby he would be discharged as unfit. He decided to feign madness. Little by little he would absent himself from his unit, first one day at time, and then for several days consecutively. When he was questioned about where he had been, he would tell his inquisitors 'I've been talking with Donatello in the woods'. Having looked up Donatello, and having discovered that he had been dead for several centuries, the authorities decided to transfer Pablo to a mental asylum for psychiatric examinations. Pablo told us, somewhat gleefully, that he then started to read every book upon which he could lay his huge hands, which dealt with psychiatric examinations and insanity in general. Eventually he was called before a board of military doctors, who subjected him to most of the standard questions he had been anticipating. 'What does the word "blue" suggest to you?' 'Cheese' replied Pablo with a perfectly straight face (or so he told us). His gamble paid off, and he was in due course discharged from the army as being psychologically unfit for any kind of duties. 'It nearly drove me mad', he recounted with a wry smile. Subsequently he managed to obtain employment as a caretaker at his Mecca, the Slade School of Art, and was eventually enrolled as a student. A far cry from our bohemian nights at Clapham Common, Eduardo Paolozzi is now recognised as one of the greatest sculptors of the age and his work is exhibited at museums and art galleries throughout the civilised world.

Lindsay and I gradually began to drift into Soho life and would frequent the streets and bistros of a tiny world of aspiring poets and painters (oddly enough, there were very few musicians) following in the footsteps of Verlaine and Rimbaud, who had frequented precisely the same corner of London some hundred years before. Our lives gradually took on a fairly regular pattern. Having worked all day at our respective obsessions (in my case, composing music) we would gravitate to where we felt we could best relax among those of our own kind. No rendezvous were ever agreed upon; we would simply arrive and drift from pub to pub (the area was relatively small and confined to a few key drinking-holes and clubs) until we met up with our regular cronies; in my case a crazy young poet and two Scottish painters, Robert

Colquhoun and Robert McBryde (invariably known as 'the two Roberts'). All were heavily addicted to cigarettes and alcohol – any sort of alcohol, but preferably whisky – but they managed nevertheless to produce a considerable corpus of works of great quality and originality. After one particularly boozy weekend, McBryde presented me with an example of his friend's work, rolled-up in newspaper and tied with string. 'Keep it', he said, 'it's a first lithograph by Colquhoun and one day it will be worth a lot of money'. Without ever opening it, I kept it for many years and when, finally, needing pictures to decorate the walls of my house, I took it to be framed, I was questioned about its origins and informed that it was now considered to be an item of some value. I subsequently lent it to an art gallery which was mounting a retrospective exhibition of Colquhoun's work and was offered a surprising sum for it by a prospective buyer. I refused. Robert was my friend. The same lithograph retains a place of honour to this day at my house in the country. At its last evaluation it was considered to be worth several thousands of pounds.

The *modus operandi* of those Soho evenings was always the same. None of us had any money and whoever had managed to sell a painting, or to publish a book of poems, or had received a commission for a musical composition, would 'be in the chair' and buy the drinks on that particular evening. It was a crazy way of life, built on dreams and excesses, and it took its toll. One of our companions, a gifted and original young painter called John Minton, penniless like the rest of us, was 'taken up' by Sir Alfred Munnings, a leading figure among the establishment and, at that time, president of the Royal Academy. Noted for his numerous portraits of horses, he invited Johnny to stay with him at his country home, where he proceeded to lecture him on the flaws inherent in contemporary art and recommended him to try his hand at 'something more conventional'. Johnny subsequently produced a painting depicting the Death of Nelson which was exhibited to considerable acclaim at the Royal Academy. But Johnny, ultra-sensitive and a chronic depressive, felt that he had betrayed himself and, not long after, committed suicide.

I only met Dylan Thomas once and he was then so incoherently drunk that I cannot say we made much contact. But, as an ardent admirer of his poetry, his early death was for me a tragedy. He had made a brilliant and innovative contribution and will surely be remembered as one of the great voices of our age. Others were not so fortunate and simply sank into poverty and obscurity.

Some lived to a ripe old age and ended up as millionaires. Francis Bacon is a name that springs to mind. A close friend of Colquhoun and McBryde and, by proxy, one of my own associates, he would invite us back to his tiny house in Notting Hill Gate, after an evening of carousing in Soho, where our discussions would continue into the small hours of the morning, cloistered within the walls upon which he habitually mixed his paints. In spite of his phenomenal success later on, Francis never wavered in his total dedication to his art, and never altered his way of life. He bequeathed his paintings, together with the many millions they had earned him, and which he never spent, to his current boy-friend, and the tiny house in Notting Hill Gate is now, I believe, preserved as a museum.

Less close to us, but a young man conscious of his saturnine good looks, much given to wearing striking and original clothing, Lucien Freud, was the grandson of the great German psycho-analyst. Ambitious and determined, he too has become a cult figure and has accumulated considerable wealth. We found him a rather aloof character and, although he never formed part of our intimate circle, we never doubted that he would fail to be left behind on the rush for glory. Nor was he. His considerable talent has ensured him his place in Elysium.

# V – Twilight Years (1954 – 1956)

Thanks to having found a more or less permanent home in Suffolk, where I could write without pecuniary anxieties, I found the bohemian life becoming less and less attractive, and creative work gradually came to dominate my whole existence. I found myself writing more and more and, since Britten had moved to Aldeburgh, only some three miles or so from where I was living, I continued to benefit from his advice and criticism. We would meet almost every day, often lunching together, and on occasions, he would play to me what he had been writing that morning. I well remember him playing me 'When as the rye reach to the chin', from the *Spring Symphony*, which he had composed that same morning, and remarking delightedly that 'It's all come out rather strangely'. Sometimes we would listen together to performances on the radio. I recall the evening we spent together listening to *Wozzeck*. Berg was another composer he greatly admired, although he had little time for Schoenberg. 'He was less of a composer than a musical scientist', he told me. 'It took an artist of the stature of Berg to make sense of the 12-tone system in order to create really valid music'. Schoenberg, had he ever come to learn of this perceptive piece of analysis, would have been less than happy. On the occasion of Stravinsky's 70th birthday, Boosey and Hawkes, his publisher, decided to devote the whole of one issue of their monthly magazine *Tempo* to Stravinsky's work, describing him as '... the greatest living composer'. They promptly received a curt telegram from Schoenberg: 'Ich lebe nur' (I am still alive). But then, as his music bears witness, a sense of humour was never Schoenberg's strongest point.

I have mentioned in a previous chapter how, in 1952, I had taken on far more work than I was able to cope with. After a particularly onerous three months striving (and only just succeeding) to meet deadlines, the inevitable happened: the machine collapsed. The result was a major nervous breakdown, which had the curious effect of leaving me totally incapable of listening to music, even to the extent of being unable to distinguish the pitch of one note in relation to another. For a while I refused to accept what had happened to me and continued to try to force myself to compose by turning day into night with the help of stimulant drugs. This, of course, only made matters worse, and my mental health deteriorated rapidly.

Finding it impossible to pursue my chosen vocation, and in order to earn enough money to keep body and soul together, I took a job as a studio attendant in the manual workers division of the BBC. In retrospect the two years which followed were horrible to live through, although richly rewarding in humans terms. My co-workers, all drawn from the humblest echelons of society, proved to be marvellously supportive whilst being, at the same time, entirely without sentimentality or pity. I learned how 'the other half' lived. Perhaps the hardest thing to bear was the constant coming into contact with artists and musicians that I had known in my previous life. Seeing me dressed in my grey dustcoat, sweeping out studios, their reactions ranged from the incredulous, through the sympathetic, to outright embarrassment.

There were, however, compensations. After much pleading, I was given unrestricted use of the music studios in Broadcasting House, where, being unable to sleep, I spent many hours – whole nights even – working at my piano technique and making experiments in acoustics. The studios were, at that time, equipped with a variety of movable panels. These I would employ to give solitary piano recitals, all the time varying the sounds I was producing by altering the position or façades of my screens. A flat, matt surface would deaden the sound, whereas a curved shiny surface would produce a brilliant resonance, even an echo. These simple experiments taught me a great deal about the art of acoustics: knowledge which was to prove invaluable later on in my second career as a chorus master. I found myself able to assess with considerable accuracy the acoustical potential of any given rehearsal premises or concert hall.

But I was unhappy. Desperately unhappy. This period in purgatory finally ended when I remembered the advice given to me by my piano teacher, Kathleen Long, when I was at the Royal College of Music. 'If ever you find yourself in real trouble', she had said, 'go along and see the Dominicans. They'll sort you out!' Motivated by a film of Graham Greene's *The Heart of the Matter*, I decided I could no longer fight against the spiritual hunger which, I now realised, had come to consume me. At nine o'clock in the evening I knocked at the door of the Dominican Priory in Hampstead and announced 'I want to become a Catholic!' The lay brother who had answered the door led me to a tiny room which, I was to learn afterwards, was known as 'The Cooler'. In due course a priest arrived, listened to my request, looked at his watch and said wryly 'Well, it's a bit late. You'd better come back and see me on Thursday'. Probably rather to his surprise, I *did* go back on Thursday, and there began a six-month course of instruction which enlightened and humbled me. In due course I was received into the Church, and Kathleen Long together with Rosemary Duncan (the wife of Ronald Duncan, author of *This Way to the Tomb* and librettist of *The Rape of Lucretia*), jointly acted as my godmothers. It was the great turning-point in my life and a decision which I have never regretted. Eventually I was allowed to go and live with the community of 24 Dominican friars and worked first as 'back kitchen man' (peeling potatoes, scrubbing floors, and feeding 'the poor men', who would congregate at the back-yard door each day after lunch) and, subsequently, as cook. Fortunately I loved cooking (although I had never previously been required to prepare three meals per day for a community of 24 friars) and I took considerable delight in offering fillet steaks, roast duck, spaghetti Bolognese, etc, to men who had become inured to the army-style fare of my predecessor. As they filed solemnly from the refectory, after a particularly tasty luncheon, hands arched before them in ritual prayer, a few would manage to pass near enough to the hatch leading into the kitchen to murmur 'Thanks, Arthur; well done...'

I now had 'a set of rails' upon which my life could run and gradually, very gradually, I began to recover my physical health and my mental equilibrium.

One day I decided to go along and see Father Agnellus Andrew, head of Catholic religious broadcasting at the BBC, with whom I had struck up a friendship during my days as a studio attendant, and for whom I had occasionally conducted small groups of singers. 'I think that I am ready to return to music' I told him. 'Is there any way in which you can help me?' By a curious co-incidence he had been talking to the Archbishop of Edinburgh that very morning, and had learned that he was looking for a choirmaster to take over the music at his cathedral. He recommended me to apply for the post and, following an interview, I was duly appointed.

# VI – The Edinburgh Cathedral Choir
## (1956 – 1971)

The choir which I inherited at St Mary's Cathedral consisted basically of 24 boys and men, some of whom had already resigned out of loyalty to my predecessor, whose contract had been terminated.

Inevitably there was opposition to my appointment, made considerably worse by the fact that I was an Englishman and therefore, by definition, 'the Auld Enemy'. Ignoring this, I immediately began to recruit new singers and rapidly built up my forces to some 40 strong. Being rather lonely at first (it was a good six months before any of the men would say more than 'Good evening' to me!) and, I must admit, partially in order to placate the fierce nationalistic pride of my choristers, I began to study early Scottish polyphonic music, much of which only existed in manuscript form and had never been performed in modern times. I spent long and happy hours teaching myself to decipher medieval notation and in transcribing the relevant part-books (full scores, inscribed upon wax tablets, had only been used at the moment of composition and then immediately erased). These works, many of them of superb quality, were gradually incorporated into the repertoire of the choir and performed liturgically at High Masses on Sundays and feast days, culminating with several performances of the magnificent 19-part motet *O Bone Jesu* of Robert Carver. Works by Palestrina, Victoria, the three Masses of Byrd, etc, together with plainchant, formed the bulk of our repertoire, which was invariably sung *a cappella*, and I gradually came to dispense with the use of the organ, using it only for accompanying hymns. The reputation of the choir began to spread and soon music students from the university were being sent to the only place where they could hear the great polyphonic repertoire being performed in its liturgical context. Remember, this was long before the New Baroque Movement had taken hold.

It was during these early days in Edinburgh that, in order principally to augment my somewhat meagre salary, I accepted an invitation from an isolated community of Cistercian monks, living near to the tiny village of Nunraw, tucked away in the Lammermuir hills outside Edinburgh, to visit them on a regular basis with a view to improving their singing of the plainchant liturgy. I would arrive on a Wednesday to give them a lesson, stay the night, and give them a further lesson the following morning. For the purposes of our classes the monks were dispensed from their rule of silence, and their naïve enthusiasm came to delight me. On one occasion I was asked by a member of the community if I considered it advisable for him to sing louder than his neighbours in order to obviate errors and to help maintain pitch. 'By no means,' I told him. 'On the contrary, you should always regulate the dynamic level of your own singing in order to blend with the others, and *never* allow your own voice to stand out.' The considerable amusement this answer evoked was explained to me later by another monk. 'It was not the chap who asked the question whose voice stands out,' he told me, 'it's the chap who stands next to him.' He went on to inform me that this technique is known in monastic life as 'scoring a cannon off the cush'. We eventually succeeded in making quite a good recording of their solemn *Salve Regina*, which they sung every evening before going to bed, and it sold many copies in their souvenir shop. In time I was accepted as an ex-officio member of the community and was allocated my own cell in the monastery instead of staying in their guest house. Many and often have these same holy men, by their humility and understanding, been a source of comfort and healing to me in the darker moments of my life.

During my years at St Mary's I contributed a considerable number of items to the cathedral repertoire, including a Mass in honour of St Thomas More (a hero of mine whose life will, I hope, one day provide me with the subject for an opera), many motets, and pieces for ceremonial occasions. I wrote a cantata, *Laudes Creaturarum* (the great poem of St Francis of Assisi) and composed, produced, and conducted a musical, *The Land of Green Ginger*, for the school at which I was teaching. Unfortunately I omitted to ask Noel Langley, author of the book on which I had based my libretto, for permission to make use of his work. It was only after a riotous first performance that I remembered to do so. He (Langley) wrote me an irate letter from Hollywood, not only refusing me permission to adapt his book, but prohibiting any further performances. The musical was consigned to the archives.

Each Edinburgh Festival the Cathedral choir would make a special effort to perform works of outstanding quality or originality (we were the first to introduce the Britten *Missa Brevis* to Scotland) and it was after one of these special Sunday High Masses that a group of excited young choirboys came rushing into my office saying 'Sir, sir, there's an important-looking man coming up the stairs'. This was to be my very first encounter with Carlo Maria Giulini. He told me that he had been present at the Mass and he complimented me warmly on our performance of Palestrina's *Missa Papae Marcelli*. He added that in his native country he no longer had the opportunity to hear such works performed and that this had doubled his pleasure on this occasion. I little realised that, over the course of the next 30 years, he and I were to collaborate in performances of all the major works in the choral repertoire and that this great man would become my close friend and mentor.

My choir of boys was called upon by the Edinburgh Festival authorities whenever a particular work demanded their participation and the men were often invited to reinforce other choirs. It was thus that I came to encounter Alexander Gibson, at that time conductor of the Scottish National Orchestra. A fine man, and a gifted musician, Alex could, at times, be temperamental and difficult to work with.

During the interval of one particular rehearsal, in which my cathedral men were participating, he called me into his dressing-room at the Usher Hall. 'What's wrong with your choir?' he asked me. 'They are so uncooperative.' Without thinking for a moment of the implications of what I was saying, I replied quite calmly '*You* are what's wrong with my choir. You have been badgering them and upsetting them throughout the whole first half of this rehearsal'. He looked at me in utter astonishment for having dared to criticise him in such a forthright manner, but he resumed the rehearsal with a changed attitude and all went well. Although I did not realise it at the time, I had personally learned a valuable lesson: always to be honest with conductors even at the risk of suffering a tongue-lashing (which fortunately did not happen on this occasion; Alex, was far too nice a human being). Over the course of a long career I have come to realise that many conductors, even the greatest among them, are very insecure people who are often surrounded by sycophants only too willing to deliver false compliments when the truth, or even silence, would have served a more useful purpose.

# VII – The Edinburgh Festival Chorus (1965 – 1977)

It was Alex Gibson who telephoned me late one evening in 1965 to ask me to meet him in Glasgow the following morning since he had an important project to discuss. It appeared that the resident choir of the Edinburgh Festival had fallen into disfavour, notably with Klemperer, who had declared he would never work with it again. The Festival director, Lord Harewood, had therefore decided to create an indigenous Scottish Chorus and, accepting the advice of Gibson and others, was proposing to put me in charge of the project. The work selected for the inaugural performance of the new chorus was Mahler's Eighth Symphony, a score of monstrous proportions demanding two huge choruses and a vast complement of boys' voices. With all the temerity of youth, I agreed, and immediately set about auditioning hundreds of amateur singers throughout the length and breadth of Scotland. It became apparent that our greatest potential would lie in three principal areas and I therefore decided to rehearse the choir in groups based upon Aberdeen, Glasgow, and Edinburgh. It was also vitally important to engage a first-class rehearsal pianist and in this I was singularly blessed in finding Michael Lester Cribb, a superb accompanist, and the musical director of Fettes College. He remained with me, loyal, discreet, and always ready with sound advice when it was needed, for the whole of my some 30 years' association with the Festival Chorus.

Having selected 240 adults and 100 boys (sufficient to fill to capacity the Usher Hall platform and to compete on equal terms with Mahler's huge orchestra) we began rehearsals. Although nowadays in the repertoire of many great choirs and conductors, the Eighth Symphony was barely known at that time and had only received one previous performance in Great Britain (under Sir Henry Wood, in the 1930s, in an English translation). I suppose that it should have been a daunting task, but it was not. The music was so glorious, so incredibly well-written for the voices and so original, that the enthusiasm of my vast army of singers carried all before it and virtually assured the success of the opening concert of the 1965 Edinburgh Festival.

Harewood decided to retain the chorus as a permanent entity and to repeat the work the following year, together with a number of others, and to invite other conductors to work with us.

In our third year Herbert von Karajan was engaged to appear with his prestigious Berlin Philharmonic Orchestra. He proposed a performance of the Bach *Magnificat*. I naturally wanted to find out all I could about his interpretation of the work and, if possible, even to meet him in order to discuss it. Impossible. Karajan's awesome entourage precluded the writing of letters, answering the telephone, or even replying to telegrams. I was particularly concerned as to whether he would want to perform the work in 'German' Latin or in the more usual 'Italian' Latin. Fortunately my friend Gibson, on a visit to Berlin, managed to secure from the German radio authorities a pirated recording of the *Magnificat* with Karajan conducting. Musically this was of enormous help to me, although I was still unconvinced by his use of 'German' Latin since, in most countries outside Germany, 'Italian' Latin was accepted as the norm. I decided to prepare my choir in both versions.

When Karajan duly arrived to take his piano rehearsal with the choir, I was first  presented to him in an ante-room. I immediately asked him which version of the Latin he would be using. 'Which have you prepared?' he asked. 'Both', I replied. 'Which do you prefer?' 'Personally I prefer Italian Latin', I replied. 'Very well then', he said, 'we will do it in Italian Latin' and he informed his soloists accordingly. Once having rid himself of any possible spectators and having locked the doors and posted his *gauleiters* outside, Karajan settled down to rehearse with a disarming simplicity. At the end of an hour he pronounced himself satisfied and, having first complimented me, told me, in his fractured English, 'I would like to take you me with'. The following day he gave a press conference at which he declared 'I made more progress with this choir in one hour that I make with most choirs in two weeks. This is one of the three great choirs of Europe'. (The other

48

two were, of course, the Singverein of Vienna and the Philharmonia of London, both trained by my illustrious predecessor Wilhelm Pitz.)

The attitude of the music critics which, while conceding the quality of the chorus, had been fairly patronising up until then, changed abruptly. The Master had spoken. From then on we were no longer 'a good local choir, doing their best' but, as Peter Diamand once stated, 'Scotland's greatest indigenous contribution to the Edinburgh Festival'.

Many fine concerts followed and, as Festivals succeeded, Diamand, by then director, proposed to me two performances with Giulini: the Schubert E flat major Mass and the Britten *War Requiem*. Once again I needed to discuss these works with the conductor and once again I encountered problems. Nobody would give me Giulini's address and I was informed that he was far too busy to meet me. I decided to go behind the backs of the authorities and I telephoned Giulini's agent in London. Having explained why it was so important to me to meet the maestro, the agent gave me his private telephone number and I rang him in Italy to request a meeting. Far from being annoyed, he seemed delighted that I should be taking the preparation of our concerts so conscientiously and he agreed to meet me in Rome. I drove to Venice, and then flew to Rome, where Giulini emerged from a rehearsal of *Cosi Fan Tutte* at the opera house and took me to lunch at his home. He asked me if I had ever performed either of the two works. 'The *War Requiem*, yes,' I replied, 'the Schubert, no'. 'Well, for me it is the opposite', he said, 'so you tell me all about the *War Requiem* and I will tell you all about the Schubert Mass'. A delightful working session followed at which I was able to obtain all the musical information I needed to begin preparing my singers adequately for their first encounter with the great man. Unfortunately, Giulini informed Peter Diamand of our meeting and in due course I received a vitriolic letter from the latter for having so successfully managed to circumvent his authority. But I did not mind. By this time I was beginning to develop a thick skin and, in any case, to be in possession of information vital to good performances was to me far more important than to be in disfavour (temporarily, as it proved) with my Festival director.

The performance of the *War Requiem* proved to be one of the greatest and most memorable occasions of my musical career. In addition to preparing the main chorus, I conducted my Cathedral boys, while Britten himself conducted the chamber orchestra with the original cast of soloists: Vishnevskaya, Fischer-Dieskau, and Pears. One greatly respected writer told afterwards of having walked 'tear-blinded into the night' when the last notes of this extraordinarily moving masterpiece had died away. I think that all of us who were privileged to participate in that evening shared his sentiments.

My first encounter with Abbado also took place in Rome. We were to collaborate in a symphonic concert (Vivaldi and Stravinsky) and also in several staged performances of Donizetti's *I Capuletti ed I Montecchi*. It is amusing to note that in this opera there are two tenor roles. The principal one was taken by Luigi Alva and the secondary one by a relatively unknown, reasonably slim, young man called Luciano Pavarotti.

Abbado proved to be possessed of a formidable talent and an undeniable charisma. But when he told me, at that first meeting in Rome, that our production in Edinburgh was to be the fourth in a series of six of the same opera he would be performing throughout Europe and in Canada that year, I could not help but ask myself who served best the art of music: the Gibsons of this world, who stayed put with their orchestras the whole year round and varied their repertoire from week to week, in order to nourish and maintain the interest of their regular audiences, or the privileged few like Abbado, who, specialising in a perfected but restricted number of works, performed them to great acclaim (and for huge fees) throughout the civilised world.

It would not be possible to imagine a greater contrast between the personality of Giulini, with whom I was now working on a regular basis, and that of Leonard Bernstein. The former would always arrive alone before an important concert, totally absorbed in the music he was about to perform, whilst Lenny would breeze in surrounded by cohorts of managers, agents, and public relations executives, most of whom seemed to have one common aim in life: to fawn upon the maestro and to flatter him whenever an occasion presented itself. At our first rehearsal of Mahler's Second Symphony with the chorus, he began by coming straight over to where I was playing the piano to 'warm up' the voices and kissing me on the top of my bald head. A rather shocked silence followed. This kind of flamboyant gesture may have gone down well in the States, but it was hardly guaranteed to win over the more reticent Scots. In addition, Bernstein spent a considerable time not only explaining the music (which I had already done) but also the *mystical implications* of the music. It proved to be a pretty boring rehearsal.

The actual performance was a circus, with Lenny leaping high into the air at the *luft-pause* in the finale and then crashing down noisily onto the podium, but it was a huge success with the audience and elicited an endless number of curtain calls in which I, as the chorus master, was inevitably involved. Many of these calls were taken by Lenny alone and each time he returned to the wings there was a young lady holding (can you believe it?) a *golden* chalice containing whisky, and a young man with a black velvet cape to drape over the maestro's shoulders during the few seconds he was in the wings. Eventually he invited the soloists and me to take a bow with him, saying 'Come on, all of you, this is everybody's show!" 'You could have fooled me' said Janet Baker, *sotto voce*.

After the performance the whole shooting match, orchestra, choirs, soloists, and conductor, were shipped off to Ely cathedral, where we spent the best part of a week together making a television film of the work. A fortnight later I dropped in to see Bernstein, who happened to be rehearsing in Vienna. He failed to recognise me.

One strange and curiously moving incident from these Festival Chorus years concerns my one and only encounter with Sir John Barbirolli. Having been engaged to perform the Beethoven Ninth Symphony with him for the opening concert of the Festival, we arranged to meet in London in order to discuss his interpretation of the score. My conception of the role of chorus master has always been that I should strive to give the conductor what he wants and not that I may think he should want. But on this occasion I questioned his interpretation concerning the duration of one particular note. It occurs at the moment when the *Allegro* changes suddenly to *Poco Adagio* halfway through the choral finale. Barbirolli felt it should be a short note, in conformity with the previous tempo, while I felt it should be long, since the slower tempo begins from that particular moment. However, I naturally acceded to his wishes and undertook to prepare the chorus accordingly. Shortly afterwards, and prior to the Festival, I took my family on holiday to Austria. Relaxing in the sunshine, far from home, I was shocked to read in my English newspaper of the sudden demise of Barbirolli, made all the more painful since my meeting with him had revealed a warm and endearing personality, easy to talk to and deeply committed to music-making in its best sense. Upon arriving home in Edinburgh I discovered a letter waiting for me on the doormat. It was from Barbirolli, and in it he said that he had had time to reflect upon our conversation and had decided to 'try it your way'. The letter, which I subsequently lent to a journalist planning to write a biography of the conductor (but who never returned it), was like a message from beyond the grave.

I celebrated the tenth anniversary of my Festival Chorus by composing a large-scale choral and orchestral work: *Psalms in Time of War*. With many double choruses and tunes which were enjoyable to sing (and, I hoped, to listen to), my singers thoroughly enjoyed rehearsing the piece – which had been one of my principle objectives. With Alex Gibson conducting, and the baritone solo being beautifully sung by Thomas Allen, the work was given an enthusiastic reception at the opening concert of the 1977 Edinburgh Festival. But I was not happy with certain aspects of the music (I decided it was a bit bombastic and overscored – too many cymbal clashes!) and I withdrew the piece from circulation. Some six years later I rewrote it entirely. It was an exercise which set my musical conscience at rest.

# VIII – Scottish Opera (1964 – 1974)

Almost co-incidentally with the creation of the Festival Chorus, and due to the genius and drive of Alexander Gibson, ably aided and abetted by a brilliant administrator, Peter Hemmings, Scotland took the bold decision to found its own national opera company. Beginning with a repertoire of only two operas in its first season, the company, an immediate success, rapidly expanded to a point where it not only mounted a complete *Ring* cycle, but also the first complete performance ever of Berlioz's greatest masterpiece *The Trojans*. Colin Davis, who was present, was to conduct the second-ever series of complete performances of this work one year later at the Royal Opera House. It is curious to reflect, in retrospect, upon the almost total oblivion which overcame the works of Berlioz after his death (an oblivion which he himself predicted in his *Memoirs*). Although his native France acknowledged his existence by putting his portrait on its ten-franc bank notes, his music was very rarely performed and few of his greatest compositions ever saw the light of day until well after the major revival which took place in the 1960s thanks to Davis's enterprise and foresight. Happily this situation has now changed and the Millenium will see all his works performed by the Orchestre de Paris in collaboration with my own current chorus. Also, in the year 2003, Berlioz's remains will be ceremoniously transferred from the cemetery in Montmartre to the Pantheon, the first musician in the history of France to be so honoured. Davis will conduct the *Symphonie Funèbre et Triomphale* as the cortège proceeds through the streets of Paris. Justice will finally have been done to France's greatest composer.

In the third year of its existence, Scottish Opera proposed to me the post of chorus master. It was an offer which I accepted with joy since, from my schooldays onward (when I had made my operatic debut as the coloratura soprano in Mozart's *Impresario*), throughout my College career, taking the leading role in theatre productions and, obviously, through my work with the Rambert Ballet Company, I had been continually associated with the theatre and had come to feel thoroughly at home with stage work and with all the excitement which accompanies rehearsals, productions, and first nights.

The chorus, when I inherited it, consisted of some 60 to 80 amateur singers, many of whom were of an extremely high quality, used to singing solo roles, and even capable of pursuing a professional career with success. Why, therefore, did they not do so? It was clearly a conscious decision based upon the uncertainties of musical life as compared to their own vocations. Indeed, some of my choristers were making a very good living at what they were already doing and had no desire to put themselves and their families at risk by plunging into a world fraught with rivalries and, let's face it, requiring more than a modicum of good luck. So they remained amateurs and came to me blessed with splendid voices and, above all, with an enthusiasm which money could never buy.

In due course, attributable to the success and to the rapid expansion of the opera company to a point where regular tours were being undertaken, this situation had of necessity to evolve. Beginning with a dozen or so professionals who worked alongside my amateur singers, the chorus eventually became wholly professional. The change-over was not easy. The amateurs resented the presence of professionals among them, and the professionals tended to despise the amateurs as more than slightly mad for not demanding pecuniary remuneration for all the hours of work they contributed. This undeclared war meant that neither group would speak to the other and that each demanded separate dressing-rooms for performances. It taught me a harsh lesson. Professionals and amateurs are like oil and water, they do not mix. It led to a policy (either one or the other, but never both together) which I have pursued ever since.

# IX – The London Symphony Chorus (1969 – 1977)

One of my more felicitous encounters during my period as Edinburgh Festival Chorus director had been with the Hungarian-born Istvan Kertesz. At that time principal conductor of the London Symphony Orchestra, he and I had collaborated in a performance of Kodály's *Psalmus Hungaricus*. Impressed with my mastery of the Hungarian pronunciation, and delighted by the Festival Chorus's performance, he proposed to me the post of chorus master to his London orchestra. Following a number of problems and misunderstandings, his current chorus master's contract had been terminated. Once again I found myself in the unenviable position of having to succeed a man who, in spite of his disagreements with authorities, retained a fierce loyalty among his troops. This was made abundantly clear to me at my first encounter with my new choristers. The work chosen for my debut was Mahler's Second Symphony, to be conducted by Abbado.

Straight away I encountered problems when the basses informed me that they had nobody capable of singing the very low B flat (*Auferstehn, ja auferstehn*) with which the choral intervention begins. 'We always engage professionals to boost the chorus', they told me, 'and it is *they* who provide the low B flat'. 'Well, I don't believe in mixing professionals with amateurs', I replied, 'so you'll just have to practice until you *can* sing it'. And sing it they did.

This particular work has always been a nightmare for choruses (and chorus masters!) because the voices are obliged to remain silent during one hour of instrumental music before entering *a cappella* and as softly as possible. Throughout the rehearsals, Abbado had systematically made a 'fermata' (an unlimited pause) in the bar preceding the entry of the chorus. At the actual performance he failed to do so. Instead, he continued to conduct: 'One, two, three, four', throughout the silent bar. Nobody, but nobody, sang. He continued to beat 'five, six, seven, eight' before a small handful of brave souls, obviously not wishing the performance to last all night, and willing themselves to avoid a disaster,

55

begin timidly to sing. One by one the others joined in and the situation was saved. The following day the press was unanimous in its praise of the chorus's contribution, and of this entry in particular. 'Never have we heard it sung so softly and with such an other-worldly sense of mystery', the critics enthused.

This strange and unnerving incident had its positive side. A bond, slender at first, began to be forged between myself and my singers. Together we had survived a potential catastrophe. However, the difficulties in our relationship persisted for many years, due in part to the fact that I had inherited a chorus committee which, while possessing no real authority by itself (the chorus was, at that time, entirely dependant upon the London Symphony Orchestra which had created it, and which continued to maintain if financially), was nevertheless possessed of a 'constitution' which the members themselves had drawn up, and which they protected with ferocity. Things eventually came to head when I discovered that this same committee had been negotiating performances, programmes, and even foreign tours without my knowledge. After my having read a prepared statement roundly condemning the actions of the committee, and of certain members of it in particular, the chorus was disbanded and immediately re-constituted with total authority being invested in me on behalf of the orchestra who, I must concede, had loyally supported me throughout the whole painful episode. The three principal trouble-makers left, and the remainder of the chorus pledged themselves, in writing, to the new regime. Never since have I willingly accepted the existence of a committee in an amateur chorus, considering that a chorus master, if he is possessed of sufficient natural authority, should be competent not only to take musical decisions but also to defend his choristers' interests, not only in dealing with difficult administrations, but also, when necessary, with the occasional errant whims of conductors.

Almost immediately after being appointed to my new post (at that time I still retained the directorship of my Cathedral choir, the Edinburgh Festival Chorus and Scottish Opera), I was plunged into a series of exciting projects with the orchestra's principal guest conductor, Colin Davis. Having been uniquely responsible for the great revival of interest in the works of Hector Berlioz, Davis planned to record, for the first time, the complete works of this neglected French genius who had had such a seminal influence upon succeeding generations of his compatriots whilst being almost completely ignored by concert promoters and conductors. At that time a performance of *The Damnation of Faust* would have been guaranteed to empty a concert hall. Today, thanks to the pioneering efforts of Davis, in which I was privileged to participate, the same work would be a box-office sell-out. The thrill of hearing, for the first time, the dramatic entry of the 16 timpani at the 'Tuba Mirum' in the *Grande Messe des Morts*, as we recorded it in Westminster Cathedral, will remain with me as long as I live. The Berlioz recordings were to be followed by the quasi-integrality of Mozart's church music.

Beginning at a fairly low ebb (Colin had been a keen supporter of my predecessor and, as he told me, failed to understand why the orchestra had decided to replace 'one good chorus master with another') the relationship, both musical and personal, between Davis and myself matured and blossomed over the years and today I invariably welcome with joy the prospect of our making music together.

Shortly after the tragic death by drowning of Istvan Kertesz, André Previn became our principal conductor. A brilliantly gifted musician, possessed of an ebullient sense of humour, Previn's background had precluded him from acquiring much experience with choirs. He admitted this to me quite frankly after an early piano rehearsal. 'I know what to do with an orchestra', he told me in effect, 'but I feel a bit lost when I am confronted with a choir. What do you suggest I should do about it?' I told him to go home, to mark all the various choral entries in different coloured inks and to 'throw them all the leads' at his next rehearsal. 'This is bound to make a good impression', I said. He did so and all went well the following day. An astonishingly quick learner, Previn went on to become a first-class choral conductor and together we made many recordings of works in the standard repertoire (and even of others, such as *Alexander Nevsky*, which were then just beginning to be known) and which have withstood the test of time.

The London Symphony Orchestra, when I worked with it, was without doubt the most brilliant orchestra in the English capital, ('although *we* are the most *musical*', as Rodney Friend, leader of the London Philharmonic, slyly pointed out). But it was arrogant. The players would frequently play the fool during rehearsals and had little respect for even the greatest of conductors. After recording the Beethoven Ninth Symphony (he was due to record the whole cycle) Giulini swore never to work with them again, 'not because of their lack of respect for me, but because of their lack of respect for Beethoven'. And he never has.

During my tenure as LSO chorus master I renewed my collaboration with Bernstein. He had delayed recording the Verdi *Requiem* for many years until the tenor of his choice became available. It became evident, during the first rehearsal with the soloists, that Bernstein had waited too long. The tenor's voice was not only no longer in the full bloom of its youth; it was completely finished. The members of the orchestra began to titter whenever the poor man opened his mouth, and eventually he left the rehearsal acutely embarrassed. With several performances and a recording already scheduled, a replacement had to be found rapidly. An up-and-coming young Spanish tenor, Placido Domingo, was engaged and caused an immediate sensation.

It is perhaps worth recounting, at this point, the story (possibly apocryphal) of the young Domingo's first encounter with the great Birgit Nilsson. It is said that he went back-stage, after one of her performances, to congratulate her. Having introduced himself, he is said to have confessed to her that one of his greatest ambitious was to sing together with her in an operatic production. 'Well, you'll have to hurry up, young man', she is alleged to have replied. 'Oh, come', said Domingo, and added gallantly 'I'm sure you'll be singing for many years to come'. 'Of course', said she, 'but will you?'.

My one and only collaboration with the aged but revered maestro Leopold Stokowski ('Don't underestimate him', warned Previn, 'we all learned at his feet') proved to be an unnerving experience. When I arrived at the room where we were to have our first piano rehearsal, I was shocked to find that the whole of our normal seating arrangements

58

had been altered. I demanded, rather angrily, to know who had been responsible for the change. An extremely nice young man who, it transpired, was Stokowski's personal manager, came forward and explained to me, with considerable delicacy, that it was he who had re-arranged the disposition of the choir. Instead of being grouped in a rough semi-circle around the conductor's podium in the middle of the room, the podium had been placed against a side wall with the choir seats clustered in front. The young man explained that he had been obliged to do this due Stokowski's advanced age (he was well over 90 at the time) and to the extreme fragility of his protegé. 'He will have his back to the wall', he said, 'and you and I will sit either side of him in order to be ready to catch him if the falls'. It was a sad ending to what had been a great career and the subsequent performance was, I believe, his last.

# X – The Chœur de l'Orchestre de Paris (1976 – )

Another bonus resulting from my years with the Edinburgh Festival Chorus was my first meeting with Daniel Barenboim. A musician possessed of astounding gifts (I would place him, in this respect, alongside Britten as one of the most naturally talented musicians of the century), Daniel was, at that time, just beginning to combine his career as a pianist with that of a conductor. I well remember our very first words to each other. Having tried unsuccessfully for many weeks to contact him with a view to discussing the work we were to perform together, I rang his number one day and, to my considerable surprise, he himself answered. Without thinking, I said 'Where have you been all my life?' 'Where have *you* been all *my* life?' he replied. It was a simple exchange, but it was to prove amazingly prophetic since we were destined to spend the best part of the next 20 years working closely together. In due course, and following a number of successful early collaborations, Daniel invited me to come over to Paris to try to form a new chorus for the Orchestre de Paris, of which he had been appointed musical director and principal conductor only a year previously. I was to learn that the idea of the orchestra having its own permanent chorus had been suggested to Daniel's predecessor, Solti, some years previously. Solti had dismissed it, giving as his reason '...there are no good voices in France'. This was, of course, arrant nonsense. There are good voices everywhere. It suffices to hunt them down and then to weld them into a coherent performing unit. I am happy to be able to confirm that Sir Georg Solti, as he had by then become, subsequently visited Paris on many occasions and was more than pleased to pursue a felicitous relationship with my chorus, which lasted until his death.

It was in view of this warning by Solti that I had not *guaranteed* to form a new chorus for the Orchestre de Paris, only to *try* to form a chorus. In the event, thanks to a splendidly orchestrated publicity campaign, the applications started to pour in, and I began systematically to audition, one by one, all 1,600 prospective candidates. It should be noted at this point that the choral tradition in France had suffered a serious set-back at the time of the Revolution, when, together with the abolition of ecclesiastical power, the vast majority of choirs, until then dependent upon the established church, had virtually ceased to exist. Unlike the countries of northern Europe, where a tradition of choral singing had remained unbroken since the 14th century, France at the beginning of the 19th century found herself, for all practical purposes, voiceless. Some progress was made in re-establishing choral singing, but not enough, and not quickly enough. The parity with, say, Germany, Holland, Scandinavia and Great Britain has still to be achieved, although in the last 20 years or so the situation has greatly improved.

When I began auditioning my prospective candidates for the Chœur de l'Orchestre de Paris, I discovered that some 70% of them had never before sung in a choir. Some, indeed, were manifestly unaware of what a choir was. 'What are you going to sing to me?' I asked one young man. 'Oh, I can't sing', he replied. 'I though that, if I joined the choir, you would *teach me* to sing'. Another lady, who proved to have been a ballerina many years previously, turned up to her audition wearing a pink tu-tu. 'I'm no singer', she told me cheerfully, 'but I can dance for you'. And she proceeded to give a hilarious rendition of the Habanera from *Carmen*, humming slightly off-key as she did so.

Eventually I was able to select some 240 voices and my long-suffering secretary and I went out and ate oysters to celebrate.

At my very first rehearsal I learned a number of salutory lessons. The voices were splendid and had great potential. The enthusiasm was ebullient. And there was an quasi-total lack of natural discipline. I had, in fact, acquired the tools to enable me to construct a splendid instrument, but the going would be hard. So I decided to make it fun. Even though this policy proved to be the correct one, it constantly back-fired. Since many years I have had the habit of stopping in the middle of rehearsals to relate an anecdote, or to tell a funny story. This serves as a respite from the effort of concentration and frequently manages to serve a useful purpose in helping the singers to mentally fix a point of interpretation. But these were Latins and, instead of digesting the lighter moments and then getting on with the music, they continued to roll about with unabashed glee for at least five minutes. As a result, concentration was lost, and only re-established with the utmost difficulty. Punctuality, taken for granted in most northern European countries, proved to be an even greater point of contention (it still is, after more than 20 years...). Whereas in Edinburgh or London the choristers would, for the most part, be seated with their scores open at the start of a rehearsal, in Paris the vast majority of my choristers would continue to chatter excitedly in the corridors for at least 15 minutes before drifting in happily and noisily ('God, grant me the grace to accept the things I cannot change... and the courage to change those I can...').

In time I was to learn that this ebullience, endemic to the Latin temperament, was to prove one of the chorus's major assets. Never have I known the Chœur de l'Orchestre de Paris to give a less good account of itself at an actual performance than at a dress rehearsal, and frequently it has delighted and astonished me by not only rising to the occasion but often surmounting obstacles with a totally unexpected ease and assurance. Performances bring out the best in these singers and the previous lack of concentration is transformed into total commitment.

Our inaugural programme was scheduled to be the Berlioz *Te Deum* in the magnificent basilica of St Eustache, where the work was given its first performance. During one of the final rehearsals we returned from the entr'acte to discover, much to the orchestra's delight, a very drunken tramp seated happily amongst the viola players. Since nobody, least of all the musicians, seemed disposed to do anything about the situation, I took the culprit gently by the arm and led him outside into the street. When I returned, the players said 'Did you give him any money to stay out, Arthur?' I replied that I had. 'Then he did very well', they said, 'because we paid him to come in!'

Having surmounted our first obstacle with honour, we settled down to constructing a permanent repertoire. Although both critics and audiences were united in welcoming the new choir, we nevertheless encountered a certain amount of antipathy from the existing professional choruses, which no doubt felt that our continuing existence could threaten their livelihood. Claques began to manifest themselves at our performances, booing noisily from isolated corners of the concert halls even as the rest of the audience clapped and cheered. French chauvinism reared its ugly head as posters bearing my name were defaced by slogans: 'Another foreigner!' It all made for an exciting first few months and taught me that making music in Paris was never going to be dull.

In the third year of our existence we began to undertake foreign tours, beginning with London, Washington and New York, and eventually finding our way to Berlin, Tel Aviv, Jerusalem, Japan, Italy, and even India. Life became interesting and exciting for the choir members, and we began to harvest all the best recruits at our annual auditions.

The Indian experience was, in many ways, remarkable. Having been invited to give a series of concerts in Calcutta and Delhi, within the framework of 'The Year of France in India', we began each programme with the National Anthem of our two respective countries. Conducting the series myself, I had arranged and orchestrated the Indian anthem specially for the occasional and had taught my chorus to sing it, from memory, in Hindustani. This naturally went down well with our Indian audiences, but Mozart, Fauré, and Vivaldi tended to leave them somewhat perplexed and, unaccustomed as they were to European musical influences, these same audiences even proved to be somewhat ignorant of normal concert procedures. They did not seem to know quite what to do when a piece ended and often an embarrassed silence would follow until I walked deliberately into 'the wings', whereupon everybody decided it was the done thing to applaud and they proceeded to do so, with gathering enthusiasm. I decided therefore that the solution was to break down the barrier, which evidently existed between stage and public, and I began to talk to them. 'Did you enjoy that?' I would say. A few timid voices would say 'Oh, yes'. 'Good, so did we. And now would you like us to play you something else?' And I would proceed to give them a simple introduction to what we were about to perform. This worked wonders and our tour came to a successful conclusion and proved to be an experience which has left a permanent mark on all of us who were privileged to participate.

It was in Calcutta that a small group of my choristers came to tell me that they had been to visit Mother Teresa's Mission. They had talked to her nuns and told them why we were there. One of them, who had been a professional musician before joining the order 14 years previously, and who had since heard no classical music, had expressed disappointment at not being able to attend our concert since, under their rule of strict enclosure, such excursions were not allowed. I immediately agreed to my choristers' suggestion that we should take our music to the Mission instead. We hastily improvised a programme of Bruckner motets and some chamber music and duly performed it in the small courtyard, the overlooking galleries thronged with blue-and-white-clad sisters, and with the tiny but unmistakable figure of 'the living saint' well in evidence on the first balcony. As we began the opening notes of *Locus Iste* ('...this is a holy place...'), I was disturbed to see that so many of my choristers' eyes were filled with tears that I became convinced that they would be unable to perform at all. But of course they did. Yet another mountain, this time an emotional one, had been climbed, and yet another great experience had been shared.

1996 marked the 20th anniversary of my French chorus and, in a gesture similar to the one I had made to my singers in Edinburgh in 1977, I decided to write another large-scale choral and orchestral work especially for the choir and Orchestre de Paris. For some ten years I had been puzzling over the poems of the 15th-century poet François Villon. Gradually I began to comprehend the archaic text and to admire the poetry more and more. It seemed to me to possess a timeless quality. Villon's humanity, his delineation of character, his sense of humour, and his ruthless honesty with regard to himself and to those around him, seemed to me to be not only relevant to the society in which he lived but also to the present day. Convicted of murder, imprisoned, and sent into exile, he died in obscurity.

Eventually I selected eight of his poems, which I welded into a coherent whole for three soloists, chamber choir, large chorus and orchestra and, borrowing his own title, called my piece *Le Testament de Villon*. The work received two initial performances at the Salle Pleyel in Paris in 1997. It was conscientiously prepared and conducted by John Nelson. One critic, in *Le Figaro*, compared it to 'the giant frescoes of Honneger'. I wouldn't go that far, but I do know that all of us who took part enjoyed ourselves (thus fulfilling one of my principal aims in writing music), and that the audiences were enthusiastic and generous in

Right: Giving instructions to the choir from a pillar of the Roman amphitheatre in Orange, France, *Samson and Delilah*, 1978. (Photo, Raymond Vennier)

Left: Sir Colin Davis with Arthur Oldham. (Photo, Raymond Vennier)

Above: The author with Daniel
Barenboim.
(Photo, Raymond Vennier)

23rd June 1975.

To the members of the
Edinburgh Festival Chorus.

I would like to thank
you again for the wonderful
days in Paris. Your courage
and determination on Saturday
were so admirable that it may
put in the background the
tremendous performance you
gave on Thursday. I don't ever
expect to hear the Ninth Symphony
sung with greater beauty, precision
or strength.
Thank you all with all
my heart. Daniel Barenboim

Right: Barenboim's letter to the
Edinburgh Festival Chorus in 1975.

Rostropovitch, the author and Jard Van Ness, *Alexander Nevski,* 1982.
(Photo, Raymond Vennier)

Arthur Oldham with Carlo Maria Giulini.

Arthur Oldham with Jessye Norman during a recording of the Berlioz *Marseillaise* at the Place, Vendome, Paris in 1986. (Photo, Raymond Vennier)

The composer at work. (Photo, Raymond Vennier)

their applause. No doubt they were surprised and relieved to hear a work by a living composer which they could understand and enjoy.

My choristers thanked me by making me a present of nine trees, which now adorn the garden of my beautiful old farmhouse in Burgundy.

# XI – Interlude: Youth Choirs and Earthquakes

Anybody embarking upon a career in music must, of necessity, be possessed of two qualities: love of the art and a boundless enthusiasm. The extent to which each person retains these qualities depends largely upon the evolution of their professional lives and the ability to surmount inevitable disappointments. Somebody once defined a saint as being 'an ordinary human being with an extraordinary gift for being able to pick himself up and start again after being knocked down'.

It is sad to see how many professional musicians, fired initially by dreams and ambitions, come to regard the practice of their art as a routine chore once they come to realise that there can only be one Heifetz in each generation. Constrained to spend day after day rehearsing the same works, frequently under indifferent or egotistical conductors, music comes to signify no more than a means of paying the mortgage. The flame of early idealism which motivated the long hours of solitary study has long since departed, only to flicker into life again when fortune presents the occasion to work with artists or conductors capable of re-awakening it. 'The day when I wake up and say to myself "... Oh! another rehearsal this morning!" will be the day I know it is time to stop', said Giulini. And his music-making, throughout a long and distinguished career, has proved his fidelity to this maxim.

On the many occasions that I have been called upon to work with young musicians, be they singers or orchestral players, I have invariably been impressed by their quasi-total dedication and by the will to work long hours striving for perfection, clearly motivated solely by love of the art of music. Not for these youngsters the surreptitious glancing at watches or the huddled conferences around the union representative during intermissions. On the contrary, the talk is all of the music they are rehearsing and of the concert to come – 'the great day'.

The European Community Youth Orchestra, founded and nurtured by the indefatigable Lionel and Joy Bryer, and privileged to spend several weeks each summer working with one or other of the world's greatest conductors, was to provide me with the opportunity to create my first International Youth Chorus. Our chosen programme included extracts from the *Sacred Pieces* of Verdi and Stravinsky's *Symphony of Psalms*. The principal conductor was Abbado and the chosen city was Rome. My chorus was made up of many elements from as far afield as Norway, Hungary, and even Colombia. After a joyful and highly successful series of performances, televised throughout Europe, I was approached by the leader of the Colombian delegation. A charming man, deeply imbued with a love of music and solicitous with regard to the development of music in his own (very poor) country, he proposed to me that I should to come to Colombia to prepare and conduct a programme of my own choice. I agreed immediately and proposed Mozart (*Exsultate, jubilate*) and the Fauré *Requiem*. The financial arrangements were simple. He would pay the air fares and hotel expenses for myself and my wife, and I would ask no fee.

When, in due course, we arrived in Popayan, in the south of Colombia, we were given a royal welcome and installed in a beautiful and ancient monastery long since converted into a quality hotel. Situated almost on the equator, we were delighted to see bananas and coffee growing everywhere, although our first experience of seeing vultures flying overhead was less agreeable.

My choristers came from different cities throughout the country and I was rapidly made painfully aware of how under-privileged these singers were. No music conservatories existed and most of the instrumental and vocal teachers had long since emigrated to the United States, where it was possible to gain a livelihood. There was only one orchestra of quality in the whole country, the Colombian National Orchestra, and this had been duly engaged to play for our performances.

Given the lack of any permanent musical infrastructure, the standard of the various participating choirs was impressive. I asked the conductor of the Medellin choir, who arrived note-perfect and sang everything from memory, how he had prepared his choir. 'Well', he replied, 'you see we don't have a pianist, so I play four bars on my violin and the sopranos sing it until they know it. Then I repeat the same four bars for the altos and so on...'. To somebody like myself, coming from Europe and with all musical means at my disposal, it was a humbling experience.

Our concerts were intended to conclude the official celebrations of Holy Week marked, each evening, by colourful processions of the relics of saints through the streets of this beautiful little town founded by the Spanish conquistadors in the 16th century, and virtually unchanged ever since.

Rehearsals went well and I managed to weld the disparate elements of my chorus into a coherent whole and even to control, to a large extent, the more volatile elements of the Colombian National Orchestra.

On the morning of the scheduled dress rehearsal my wife and I were having breakfast with our host in the Hotel del Monasterio when a noise began which exactly resembled a long crescendo timpani roll. Simultaneously we observed that the pillars of the dining room were no longer vertical but were beginning to dissolve into wavy lines. 'Terremoto!' screamed our host, and the three of us rushed out into the garden while huge chunks of masonry fell all around us. (Long afterwards we were told that what we should have done was to get under the table and stay there. But it is easy to be wise after the event and, in any case, earthquakes do not come one's way every day). The tremor lasted for 12 seconds but it devastated the town. In the basilica above, 500 people died when the building collapsed upon them as they were attending Mass.

By the grace of God all my choristers survived and joined us eventually in the monastery garden. Within hours, helicopters were landing nearby (all the streets were rubble and the runways at the tiny airport were unserviceable due to the huge fissures which had appeared). The helicopters had arrived from the United States and had brought in representatives of the International Press Corps. With the maximum of insensitivity one hard-nosed gentleman came to me and, without any preliminaries, said 'How many of your party are dead?' I sent him brusquely on his way. This did not prevent some creative journalism appearing subsequently and purporting to be exclusive interviews: 'Famous conductor screams "Where is my orchestra?" '.

In fact the orchestra, despite an impassioned plea from myself, left Popayan almost immediately by whatever transport was available, fearful, as were we all, of aftershocks.

The choir, however, decided to go ahead with our planned performance, in memory of those who had died so tragically that morning. The orchestra was replaced by an upright piano carried over the rubble on the backs of four of my choristers to the monastery garden. There, standing on a table, and surrounded by my faithful singers, I conducted the most moving performance of my life.

A year later a fine illustrated book was published entitled *Twelve Seconds in Popayan*, recounting the whole terrifying story and concluding with a photograph of our Fauré *Requiem* as we sang and prayed and, perhaps, wept.

# XII – The Concertgebouw Choir (1980 – 1986)

Having attended a performance of *Alexander Nevsky* in Paris, Bernard Haitink invited me to Amsterdam to form a new permanent chorus for his Concertgebouw Orchestra. At first all went well. The prior publicity campaign brought in well over 2,000 potential recruits and, when rehearsals eventually got under way, I experienced none of the disciplinary problems which I had encountered during my early days in Paris. The vast majority of my singers had been singing regularly in various choral groups since childhood. This helped a lot, and we able to begin concentrating almost immediately upon the musical preparation of the Ninth Symphony and the *Symphony of Psalms* which marked our debut.

The situation began to deteriorate after an unhappy first collaboration between myself and Nikolas Harnoncourt. At our first meeting he told me 'I never get on with chorus masters'. The reasons rapidly become obvious. Having risen from the ranks of the string section of the Vienna Symphony Orchestra, Harnoncourt clearly had no conception of vocal technique or interpretation, preferring to leave the choice of soloists to his agents. At an early rehearsal of the *St Matthew Passion* he told the chorus '… never pronounce the consonants at the ends of words. This introduces a percussive element into the music'. Given his background as a string player, I could appreciate how he had arrived at this extraordinary conclusion. But I could not, and would not, accept a dictum that I knew to be false and which went against a lifetime spent working with singers. The following year Harnoncourt demanded that my pianist replace me for the preparation of the *St John Passion* and I promptly resigned. Although I rather weakly went back on my decision, and continued to train the chorus for a few more years, the damage was done. Hampered by a malevolent administrator, and failing to find any support from a musical director profoundly immersed in his own personal problems, I consented to a dissolution of the choir. I am happy to be able to relate that this fine group of singers immediately reformed itself and, under the name of the Netherlands Concert Choir, continues to make a valuable contribution to the musical life of Holland.

The fact that my Concertgebouw chorus was eventually dissolved was all the more galling since during several years we had succeeded in giving first-class performances of almost all the standard works in the choral repertoire (*War Requiem*, Verdi *Requiem*, *Damnation of Faust*, etc) with many of the world's leading conductors. The problem was basically that the members of the orchestra never really accepted the presence of an amateur choir, considering that anything less than a professional group was unworthy of them. One incident confirmed this. The governing committee of the orchestra delegated one of their members (he happened to be a percussion player) to interview me with a view to giving me advice on how to train my chorus. Needless to say his advice was not only unhelpful but, frankly, ridiculous, since he, in common with many orchestral players, knew nothing about choirs or vocal technique. I listened in astonishment to what he had to say, and it would be difficult to say which of us was the more embarrassed.

Many years later I prepared the excellent Gulbenkian choir for a performance in Lisbon with the Concertgebouw Orchestra and Colin Davis. The attitude of the orchestra had clearly undergone a sea-change and we parted on extremely friendly terms after a stunningly successful concert.

Having finally broken with the Concertgebouw in 1986, I returned for a further spell to my old love, the Edinburgh Festival Chorus. Much had changed: not least the Festival itself. The brilliant and exciting Peter Diamand years were still in my memory, but the emphasis had subtly changed from music to theatre. The repertoire proposed to me was, in the main, pedestrian and, having prepared most of it many times before, I felt constantly hampered by a feeling of *déjà vu*. Happily, with the accession of Brian McMaster to the post of Festival Director, musical excellence once again became a priority and the stunning concert performance of Schoenberg's *Moses and Aaron*, which had been chosen for his opening concert, constituted the ultimate challenge for amateurs.

My chorus too had changed. Many of my old friends had left, and members who had not worked with me previously found my methods strange and difficult to accept. In spite of this we managed to regain our old confidence and to give some wonderful performances. But I was beginning to find that the constant weekly journeys between France and Scotland were more than I could cope with, and in 1994 I resigned for a second and final time. By a curious coincidence, Mahler's Eighth Symphony was back in the programme that year. For me, the wheel had come full circle.

# XIII – Paris and Barenboim

Since the majority of my years with the Chœur de l'Orchestre de Paris have been spent with Daniel Barenboim as musical director, I feel it appropriate at this stage to elaborate upon my collaboration with this remarkable musician. To those who are not given to know him closely, he may give the impression of being authoritarian and abrupt. This is quite false. As was Karajan, Daniel is obliged to protect himself from the vast army of admirers and sycophants who continually court him. It is true that he is extremely intolerant of those among his colleagues whom he finds lacking in the qualities which he deems, rightly in my opinion, necessary to achieve the best performances. I once saw him abruptly dismiss a guitarist from an orchestral rehearsal giving, as his reason for doing so, 'I can't stand people who don't prepare their work properly'. The fact that he was blessed with a prodigious talent from a very early age and grew up in a family 'where everybody played the piano' (his mother and father were both teachers) did little to attenuate this tendency towards intolerance. But the real Barenboim can be discerned when one listens to him interpret the slow movement of a Mozart piano concerto. His sensitivity and humility before the greatness of Mozart's genius is manifest.

I always enjoyed a privileged relationship with Daniel. As a proven expert in preparing choirs, he needed me as much as I needed him, and hierarchical considerations were set aside. He would frequently mock me: 'Arthur, you're full of shit!' he once told me (he had recently returned from a trip to America and was clearly delighted to air a phrase from his newly discovered vocabulary). But, when the crunch came, he revealed himself to be plagued with the same self-doubts and hesitancy as all of us who are obliged to live with an artistic temperament. One day he announced that he had decided to conduct his first *Missa Solemnis*. Beethoven's great masterpiece, with its vast emotional range and technical complexity which was once described to me by Giulini as 'The Parnassus', has terrified many conductors. A few months after having taken this decision, Daniel summoned me to his office and announced that he no longer wanted to conduct the *Missa*. He had been talking to the widow of Furtwängler and she had told him that her husband had only once conducted the work and had then renounced ever performing it again, declaring it to be 'unplayable'. I pointed out to Daniel that he had performed many times (and recorded) all the Beethoven piano concertos, the symphonies, and the chamber music, and insisted that he *must* accept the challenge of the *Missa* in spite of his doubts. 'The choir can sing it', he replied, 'but I'll engage another conductor'. I told him that this was not the answer; that he owed it to his own integrity to perform the work at least once and then if, like Furtwängler, he felt it to be impossible, his musical conscience would at least be satisfied. Having prepared the work myself on many occasions, and with many different conductors, I offered to help him as much as I could. He finally succumbed to my admonitions and asked if I would play the work through to him and talk about it.

In due course Daniel came round to my apartment, bearing a gift of a box of chocolates, and I proceeded to play through the score. It was only afterwards that I realised that I, with my modest pianistic abilities, had been performing for one of the greatest pianists of the age. At the time it did not occur to me, nor would it have inhibited me, because we were both so caught up in the greatness and excitement of the music that self-consciousness simply did not enter into it.

The performances (we began with three consecutively) were a triumph and, as we were leaving the stage together, Daniel told me to go to his dressing-room and wait for him. When he arrived, he asked me to stand beside him and proceeded to present me personally to all the visitors who flocked to congratulate him – including Furtwängler's widow. He then invited my wife and I to dine with him. It was a gracious and charming gesture which I took as an acknowledgement of the long road we had travelled together. The *Missa*, far from being set aside, went on to become a centre-piece of Daniel's repertoire and, upon acceding to the directorship of the Chicago Symphony Orchestra, he made a fine recording of the work.

# XIV – Working With Voices

My first choir of any consequence consisted of a small group of students, augmented by a few outside elements – American servicemen still stationed in Europe, one or two out-of-work professional choristers, etc – formed in 1945 in order to provide the off-stage choral commentary to Ronald Duncan's 'masque and anti-masque' *This Way to the Tomb* (see Chapter II). I look back on this experience with a mixture of pride and shame. I took pride in the quality of the work. We had assembled a fine group of semi-professional singers and we did justice to Britten's beautiful incidental music. I discovered that choir-training came easily to me and that I possessed a natural authority. But I was hated.

This was in 1945, the year when the Allies overran Europe and the horrors of the concentration camps were being discovered. It was also barely five years since the death of my father and the suicide of my mother. I was a deeply disturbed young man who compensated for his own sense of insecurity by adopting an arrogant and aggressive attitude to all over whom I was given authority. As a result, my choristers came to refer to me as the 'The Beast of Belsen'.

It has taken many many years, and much soul-searching, to realise that it is perfectly possible, indeed preferable, to obtain the same results, even better, by being nice to people. This may sound obvious and simplistic but for me it has been perhaps the greatest single lesson I have learned in my long career as a choir trainer. I can state without any doubt that for many years now I have retained the respect and even the love of my choristers without ever having to concede one whit of my authority.

Once again it was my great musical mentor, Giulini, who pointed out to me that, given the position that I occupied, I could have a vast influence, for good or otherwise, over the lives of those who worked with me. At first I was incredulous, but I came to accept that what he had told me was true. I began consciously to deepen my relationships with my singers to the extent where now they feel able to come and discuss with me anything that troubles them, not only musically but in their personal lives as well. To this end I make myself available for the half-hour preceding rehearsals, and also during the intervals, in order to be able to receive them individually and to give them whatever advice I feel might be of help. Quite apart from the knowledge that one is being of some practical use to one's fellow human beings, this approach produces great musical rewards. A singer who feels he has a personal loyalty to his chorus master will be ready to give everything to him musically. The consequences of this mutual exchange of loyalty and affection are certainly to be noticed, consciously or subconsciously, in performances.

All that I do in preparing a choir for a concert has a single *raison d'être*: to ensure the best possible result when the lights are dimmed and the conductor raises his baton. In order to achieve this end, everything is permissible. If I stop during a rehearsal in order to tell a story, or to play the clown, it is to fix a particular musical point in the minds of my 'audience'. If one feels so inclined, and if one feels it is going to help musically, one should not hesitate to assume the role of entertainer. I recall that one occasion a member of my bass section turned to the new young recruit standing beside him and said 'Have you seen Arthur's circus act before?' 'Yes', replied the young man, 'many times: I'm his son'. If I become angry, or even walk out of a rehearsal (and, on very rare occasions, I have done so), it is because I am certain in my mind that this will guarantee discipline on future occasions and that it is the only way to ensure that, when the great occasion arises, my troops will be ready.

The preparation for a concert, or series of concerts, begins for me months before the first rehearsal with a thorough study of the score of the work involved. If I should arrive ill-prepared, and God forbid I ever should, my choristers would know it instantly. I recall that, on one occasion when the London Symphony Chorus was trying out various postulants to succeed me at the termination of my mandate in 1975, they had invited a young man to prepare them for the *Missa Solemnis*. Hoping no doubt to set them (and himself) at ease, he announced breezily 'I know nothing whatever about this piece, so I hope you are going to teach me'. The horrified silence which greeted this extraordinary pronouncement was a clear indication that he had lost them – permanently. Many of those present had previously belonged to the Philharmonia Chorus and, having painstakingly prepared the work with the great Wilhelm Pitz, they considered such an attitude to be little short of *lèse-majesté*.

Over the years I have taken over the directorship of many choirs. I have also founded three: the Edinburgh Festival Chorus (1965), the choir of the Orchestre de Paris (1976), and the choir of the Concertgebouw Orchestra (1980). All these latter have been amateur choirs and this has been a conscious choice on my part. My work with professional choruses, notably that of Scottish Opera, which I directed for ten years, has never given me the deep musical satisfaction that I have experienced from working in the great North European tradition of amateur choruses. To begin with, the approach to working with a professional chorus is inevitably different. There are advantages and disadvantages. With a profession chorus you can be reasonably certain that, at ten o'clock on a Monday morning, all your singers will be present and captive for the next three hours. Work in the daytime is the norm, whereas an amateur choir, due to the business and family obligations of individual members, can only be available for rehearsals in the evenings and at weekends – a situation which is not always to the liking of the professional orchestras with whom they are called upon to perform. This can lead to tensions, usually resolved by the quality of the musical contribution of the amateurs or by tours undertaken together with the orchestra which provide an opportunity for each 'side of the fence' to get to know and, hopefully, to respect each other. Sometimes it works; sometimes not. The Concertgebouw Orchestra never really accepted the fact of having an amateur chorus sharing their performances. The orchestral players, in common with those of most orchestras, were unable to assess the merits of the chorus's contribution and clearly considered that a chorus of 'amateurs', as opposed to a professional chorus, was beneath their dignity. This ignorance of choral work on the part of orchestral players was never more obvious than in the London Symphony Orchestra, where, whenever their chorus began to sing, the first trumpet player, seated immediately in front of the choir altos, would begin conspicuously reading his Mickey Mouse comic.

Needless to say, the chorus took this as being not so much a valid piece of musical criticism as a measure of the man's ignorance of all but the little world of his particular instrument, not to mention his taste in literature.

Another vital consideration to be borne in mind by any chorus master is that his attitude when working with amateurs as opposed to professionals will inevitably be conditioned by their difference in status. The professional chorister is there primarily in order to earn his living. The amateur chorister can have no other motivation but the joy of making music. If a singer in a professional chorus fails, for whatever reason, to give satisfaction, his contract will not be renewed. No such sanction is available to those of us who choose to work with amateurs. A heavy responsibility rests upon our shoulders to make rehearsals interesting and agreeable. One must never forget that an evening rehearsal frequently follows a long and perhaps frustrating day at the office, at school (a large number of the members of amateur choruses are music teachers), or even at home. The singers come along to rehearsals to enjoy making music with their friends and, hopefully, to put the day's worries behind them for a few hours. One distinguished surgeon who sang tenor in my Edinburgh Festival Chorus said to me: 'You know, Arthur, there are only two times in my week when I feel completely relaxed. One is when I am operating, because nobody is allowed to talk to me. The other is when I come to a chorus rehearsal and somebody else – you! – tells *me* what to do'. For me, the ideal rehearsal is when the choristers leave chatting happily, having had a great evening, and when *I* leave knowing that, musically, we have made progress.

The rapport between a choirmaster and his singers must be that of the complete professional and those human elements he is attempting to mould into a coherent performing unit. *They* provide the enthusiasm and the vocal material. The chorus master has to provide the expertise. I am frequently asked if I feel frustrated when the moment arrives for me to hand over my choir to a conductor. I can honestly reply that I never feel this way because I see my role as that of an instrument maker who works not with catgut and wires but with human beings, and whose duty it is to hand over this instrument, at the appointed time, in as perfect a state as possible in order that the conductor may then weld it into the

78

great whole which makes up a corporate musical performance. A chorus, at this stage, should not only be note-perfect, and possess impeccable intonation, but also be totally flexible in order that the conductor may feel free to interpret the music as he wishes, even to the extent of changing his mind at the moment of performance. I once asked Sir Adrian Boult, for whom I was to prepare Vaughan Williams's *Dona Nobis Pacem*, how he proposed to beat a certain passage – in two, or in four. He studied the score in silence for a few minutes and then replied 'I've no idea, dear boy, just tell them to follow me and everything will be alright.'

The role of the chorus master has long been considered either as inferior (viz Gerald Moore's remarks in *The Unashamed Accompanist* which clearly prove that a similar attitude prevailed in the early days of his career, even to having the pianist hidden behind the potted palms whilst the diva occupied the centre stage) or as a stepping-stone to better things. All too many chorus masters have considered that their ultimate destiny is to become orchestral conductors. Some – very few – have succeeded. Many more have foundered on the rocks of their own ambition. There is nothing demeaning in devoting one's whole life and energies to working with voices. I have always considered it a privilege. Not only is the human voice the finest of musical instruments, but the chorus master enjoys a unique status in that he not only commands but also serves. Fortunately there is now a whole new generation of young choral directors, especially in England, who are accomplishing marvels with choirs because they have realised that a career in choral music is an honourable end in itself. This argues well for them, for their choirs, and for music in general. They are at the same time discovering that their co-operation with orchestral conductors is made easier because the latter feel more at ease working with a specialist. I have encountered many conductors who, having worked with instruments all their lives, still do not feel completely at ease with voices and who consequently depend upon people like myself to give them what they, on their own, may not have been able to have achieved.

In preparing for a major concert I have always considered it vital to discuss the score with the designated conductor some months before the conclusion of the preparatory work with the choir. Such a discussion is preferable in a face-to-face meeting, although it can sometimes be achieved by telephone. In either case such a discussion guarantees that there will be fewer surprises when the conductor eventually meets his choir, and can result in much less time being wasted at final corporate rehearsals. Not all conductors know how to rehearse economically. I have known some who will embark upon long philosophical dissertations when they should be correcting points of interpretation or making clear how they intend to beat certain difficult passages. As a result they lose the concentration of their captive listeners and simply bore them into lassitude. Others, with a minimum of verbosity, simply get on with the music and ensure themselves a safe and enthusiastic performance. Karajan was like this; so was Abbado. Claudio rarely raised his voice above normal speech-levels and yet was capable of maintaining an atmosphere of intense concentration. On the one occasion he conducted my chorus in Paris (it was for a performance of *Alexander Nevsky*), he pronounced himself satisfied at the end of 40 minutes' piano rehearsal, congratulated the choir, and went home. My singers went home too: ecstatic and confident. The concert was a triumph. Haitink was in the audience and it was shortly after this that he contacted Barenboim, my musical director, to ask permission to invite me to Holland to form a new choir for his Concertgebouw Orchestra.

Some years ago I asked my secretary to analyse the current composition of the Chœur de l'Orchestre de Paris. We discovered that we had no less than 18 different nationalities represented: people from as far afield as Japan, China, Korea, Russia, Romania, America, Ghana, Lebanon. A great chorus, especially in a metropolis such as Paris, becomes a microcosm of society. It is also a model of true democracy. Within the family of the chorus it is not the person who holds down the top job, or who earns the most money, who is the most respected by his fellows. It is the best singer. The fact that one is the managing director of a large industrial enterprise (and we have quite a few, along with doctors, schoolteachers, secretaries, journalists – even, at one time, a professional cyclist and a man who earned his living by sweeping the platforms of the Metro) counts for little once rehearsals get under way. It is those who are called upon to sing solo before their colleagues (I always choose individuals to learn and to sing in the solo parts until the professionals arrive), and who acquit themselves honourably, who become the true aristocrats. It warms my heart to observe how frequently a lonely person can suddenly discover a host of friends and admirers as a result of having sung a solo beautifully.

This social disparity should also exist vocally. Many chorus masters make the mistake, when auditioning potential recruits, of having too rigid an idea of what kind of voice they are looking for. The result is all too often a soprano section consisting entirely of 'white' voices (and therefore incapable of doing justice to the grandiose tuttis of a Verdi *Requiem*) or a tenor section consisting of aspiring Pavarottis who will never be able to come to terms with the delicacies of a Mozart Mass. Similarly, a candidate with a good singing voice should not be rejected simply because he or she does not sight-read well. Rather they should be accepted into the choir and encouraged to take lessons to help them overcome their deficiency. In my Parisian chorus we have a number of music teachers more than willing to help new recruits in this manner. One should never forget that everybody makes a contribution, though disparate, to the success of an eventual performance. During the early rehearsals it will obviously be the best sight-readers whose vocal contribution is most in evidence, but they are not necessarily the best or the strongest singers. When the evening of the concert arrives, it may well be that they are heard little, whilst those they have nurtured make the most audible impact.

Similarly, I encourage most of my singers to take regular lessons from a private teacher to improve their vocal technique, and I would estimate that 80% of my current choristers do so. I even make this a condition of entry into the choir if the candidate is an excellent sight-reader but is possessed of a small voice with the potential to improve. Not all can afford to do so, but those who can, and do, often make startling progress. A choir consisting of voices with an accomplished vocal technique, all of whom are perfect sight-readers, would make the life of a chorus master very easy. But this is a Utopian concept and, like paradise, is a goal to be striven for, not to be taken for granted. And it the striving that makes the victory all the sweeter.

Many choirs are dogged by committees. I have never accepted or approved of this system of governance, considering that if the chorus master has a sufficiently strong personality, he or she will be in a position to resolve all the problems which might arise and be able to plan intelligently and to defend his army against not only possible minor rebellions but also against recalcitrant, and often ignorant, administrations. To my mind, a choir requires no more than three human elements in order for it to succeed: a choirmaster, a secretary, and a pianist. All must be top-class and devoted to their work. Relations with any prevailing administration should be left to the chorus master, who should be prepared to defend his members' best interests with regard to suitability of repertoire, spacing of concerts, and how much can be undertaken in any given season. The administration, for its part, should be prepared to accept the advice of their choral director, who, after all, was supposedly engaged as being a competent judge in such matters.

# XV – Music at the Millennium

The advent of the third millennium of the Christian era would appear to present an excellent occasion for taking stock of the current musical scene. In over 50 years of musical *métier* I have witnessed many revolutions and evolutions. Music is now available to all. No longer is it necessary to plan one's musical forays well in advance; the whole gamut of musical activity is today at one's finger-tips. We press a button and we share in first-class musical performances, meticulously prepared for us, through the medium of television. Press another button, and we may compare superb recordings of the world's greatest artists, past and present. It could be expected that the public for live concerts would have diminished, but such is the power of music that the opposite is true. Audiences flock to concert halls in ever-increasing numbers in order to hear their favourite artists and masterpieces and all tastes are catered for. A good thing? Well, yes; but with reservations. With such a vast market, music has become increasingly commercialised. Art no longer thrives 'for its own sake' but, all too often, to fill the coffers of concert promoters and shrewd agents. There exists a shocking imbalance between the 'stars' of the musical world and those to whom it falls to pursue the more mundane tasks, and without whom music, as an art, could well cease to exist. It has been noted elsewhere that conductors are grossly overpaid. For one series of concerts in Vienna, Bernstein was reputed to have received a fee exceeding the whole of the concert fees of his orchestra put together. This is outrageous; although I suppose it never crossed Lenny's mind that without each and every member of his ensemble, from leading violinist to third percussion player, his own contribution would have been useless.

Again, the true tenor voice is a rarity and really great tenors are few and far between. But does this really justify paying colossal concert fees to the few top stars of the international circuit when, all too frequently, their performances turn out to be not only disappointing but sometimes downright shameful? Such people do not serve music; they use music to serve themselves.

This commercialisation of music has led to a situation where music is no longer judged on its intrinsic merits, but on how much it will gross at the box-office. Read any respectable daily newspaper and you will often find more space devoted to reviews of 'pop' than to assessments of classical performances and recordings. Even the Performing Right Society, once revered as a venerable institution for 'the protection of composers, authors, and arrangers', is now entirely dominated by the proponents of 'pop', to the detriment of the interests of serious musicians. Financial success has become the arbiter of what is to be performed or discussed in lengthy journalistic post-mortems.

But here we encounter another problem. It concerns the proliferation of experimental music frequently, as is the case in France, heavily subsidised by governmental agencies peopled by advisers all too frequently lacking in real musical backgrounds and whose main concern seems to be to keep pace with prevailing musical fashion. Hence the vast amount of 'new' music of widely varying quality being put before a diminishing public.

As for the composers themselves, it seems to me that many are in danger of losing their way and of ignoring what I have always believed to be the essentials of their craft. The long-suffering performers have to cope with a repertoire no longer conceived with themselves in mind. The contemporary composer all too frequently writes only for himself, and the executant is expected to follow his every whim. The result of this Gadarene rush for originality has, paradoxically, had the effect of producing a sameness in much contemporary composition. I once asked Pierre Boulez (a great musician and colleague, whom I would except unreservedly from these remarks) if he could tell which, among contemporary compositions, were of real value, and which were not. '*I* can,' he replied, 'but I don't think many others can'. He also wryly remarked that the majority of contemporary compositions received two performances only: 'the first and the last'.

Reverting for a moment to my early discussions with Britten, I recall him expressing the hope that composers might eventually come to re-adopt a common musical idiom (viz, Haydn and Mozart). Today that hope seems doomed and excessively idealistic. But rays of light are beginning to penetrate the clouds. A few composers are starting to write comprehensibly once more and, without sacrificing their own musical personalities, are producing works which performers actually enjoy performing and to which audiences can actually enjoy listening. Too many 'isms' – atonalism, serialism, minimalism – plague our contemporary musical scene and effectively disguise a lack of real creative talent. And all too few composers realise how hard it is to write down what they *actually hear*, because they will then risk exposing their own nakedness. Many prefer to don the Emperor's new clothes or to subscribe to what Britten dubbed 'the wrong-note school'. Strip away the deliberate dissonances and the mediocrity of the ideas becomes plain to all.

Many years ago a candidate presented to me a very early song by Webern for her audition. It was, frankly, an undistinguished piece of work, a sort of fourth-rate Brahms, and I could not help but reflect that, had it not been for the cabalistic and esoteric success of the Second Viennese School, Webern would not be occupying the eminent position he does today.

Nowhere is this dichotomy between performers and composers more evident than in the realm of vocal music – and of choral music in particular. Singers are constantly being asked to perform quasi-impossible feats, with the results that, all too often, only professionals who have decided to specialise in such music are able to cope with the over-complex scores with which they find themselves confronted. The result is that 'amateur' performers, who have a valid claim to consideration, find themselves excluded. During a recent performance of new work by Donatoni (which included three air-raid sirens), all six vocal soloists were obliged to use pitch-pipes or tuning forks to find their entry notes, the preceding cacophony having left them no alternative. Such things should never happen.

Another current phenomenon is the craze for trying to re-construct 'authentic' performances. From a musicologist's point of view such performances can be useful in shedding historical light on works which, as a result of many generations of accumulated 'tradition', have lost their original sheen and impact. But are these so-called 'restorations' really valid? And can we ever say, with certainty, that what we are hearing is what the composer intended us to hear, or even that he may not have been delighted to hear his musical vision expanded by modern performing resources and by the evolution of instrumental construction and techniques? We can restore the frescoes in the Sistine Chapel and re-discover, with near certainty, Michelangelo's original masterpiece. But too often only documents and contemporary illustrations are available to help us to re-construct early instruments and performances. And usually the research is done, no doubt painstakingly, by musicologists and scholars who themselves have little or no experience of practical music-making. The results can often be remarkably dull. I remember Giulini telling me of a concert he had attended in Cologne where the Bach B minor Mass was performed with a handful of voices and about 20 instruments. 'After the first ten minutes', he said, 'I was praying for a jazz band to come on and liven things up'. I experienced a similar reaction after hearing an 'authentic' performance of the Monteverdi *Vespers* at the Cité de la Musique in Paris. It was incredibly boring and I am convinced that, had it received such treatment at its première in St Mark's Cathedral, it would never have survived so gloriously for 400 years.

Fashions in composition and in performances depart as quickly as they arrive. Music survives. It always will. It supplies a fundamental need common to most human beings. Where it will lead us, and how it will evolve, none of us can tell. But the knowledge that I have been privileged to spend a lifetime in its service, in spite of having to climb a few early mountains, gives me great peace.

# Selected List of Compositions

1945    *Five Chinese Lyrics* (high voice and piano)

        *Mr Punch* (ballet)

1947    *The Sailor's Return* (ballet)

1948    *Circus Canteen* (ballet)

        *Circus Parade* (orchestra)

        *Summer's Lease* – Seven Sonnets of Shakespeare (tenor and string orchestra)

        *Variations on a Carol Tune* (chamber orchestra)

1950    *Bonne Bouche* (ballet)

        *My Truest Treasure* (SATB)

1951    *The Commandment of Love* (high voice and piano)

1952    *Four Hymns from 'Our Lady's Tumbler'* (mixed chorus *a cappella*)

        *Love in a Village* (ballad opera) (soloists and small orchestra)

1958    *Missa in Honorem Sancti Thomas Mori* (SATB chorus)

1960    Mass (congregation, choir and organ)

1961    *Rejoice, lordings* (SATB and organ)

1962    *Hymns for the Amusement of Children* (SATB, solo soprano, organ)

        *Laudes Creaturarum* (solo soprano, children's choir, mixed choir, strings and organ)

        *Regi Saeculorum Immortali* (SA)

| 1963 | Two carols (*Angels from the realms of glory*; *Remember O thou man*) |
|---|---|
| | Two hymns for the *Cambridge Hymnal* |
| | *Four Noëls* (SSA) |
| 1965 | *St Francis: Blind Audley's Carol* (SSATTB, chorus) |
| 1967 | Two hymns (*O Queen of Virtues*; *Experience does me so inspire*) |
| 1973 | Sinfonietta (wind band) |
| 1974 | *In Praise of the Virgin* (alto solo, mixed double chorus) |
| 1977 | *Psalms in Time of War* (baritone solo, mixed double chorus and orchestra) |
| 1978 | *Five Noels* (voice and flute) |
| 1984 | *Three Hebrew Melodies* (SATB, chorus) |
| 1994 | *Epithalamion* (SATB, chorus, organ, strings, or organ alone) |
| 1997 | *Cantiques des Cantiques* (soprano and flute) |
| | *Dos Villancicos de Santa Teresa de Avila* (soprano, mezzo-soprano and piano) |
| | *Le Testament de Villon* (3 soloists, chamber choir, mixed chorus and orchestra) |
| 1999 | *Cantique de Soleil* (boys' choir) |

## Arrangements

Indian National Anthem (choir and orchestra)

Dutch National Anthem (choir and orchestra)

*Simple Symphony* (Britten), version for two pianos

# Index

McBryde, Robert, 37, 38
McMaster, Brian, 71
McNeice, Louis, 29
Medellin, 67
*Memoirs* (Berlioz), 53
Mendelssohn, Felix, 9, 17
Mercury Theatre (Notting Hill Gate), 18
Michelangelo, 86
*Midsummer Marriage, A* (Tippett), 17
*Midsummer Night's Dream, A* (Mendelssohn), 17
Minton, John, 37
*Missa Brevis* (Britten), 45
*Missa in Honorem Sancti Thomas Mori* (Oldham), 87
*Missa Papae Marcelli* (Palestrina), 45
*Missa Solemnis* (Beethoven), 45, 73, 74, 76
Moore, Gerald, 20, 79
*Moses and Aaron* (Schoenberg), 71
Mother Teresa's Mission, 63
Mozart, Wolfgang Amadeus, 20, 22, 53, 57, 63, 67, 73, 81, 84
Mozart Variations, 22
*Mr Punch* (Oldham), 18, 33, 87
Munnings, Sir Alfred, 37

Nash, Heddle, 27
Nelson, John, 37, 64
Netherlands Concert Choir, 70
Nichols, Norah, 24, 26, 29
Nichols, Robert, 24
Nilsson, Birgit, 58
Ninth Symphony (Beethoven), 51, 58, 70

*O Queen of Virtues* (Oldham), 87
*Oh, for the Wings of a Dove* (Mendelssohn), 10
Old Mill, Snape, Suffolk, 5, 16, 20
Oldham, Arthur (father), 9, 10, 11, 12, 75
Oldham, Barbara (sister), 9, 10, 12
Oldham, Catherine (mother), 9, 10, 11, 12, 75
Oldham, Muriel (half-sister), 12
Orchestre de Paris, 5, 53, 60, 61, 62, 64